Traveling Home

A YOUNG MAN'S
story of courage
and FAITH

CHARLOTTE HILL &
DON WAITE

Kregel
Publications

Traveling Home: A Young Man's Story of Courage and Faith

© 2008 by Charlotte Hill and Don Waite

Published by Kregel Publications, a division of Kregel, Inc., P.O. Box 2607, Grand Rapids, MI 49501.

Library of Congress Cataloging-in-Publication Data
Hill, Charlotte.
Traveling home : a young man's story of courage and faith / by Charlotte Hill and Don Waite.
    p. cm.
Includes bibliographical references.
1. Hill, Peter James, 1977–1998. 2. Cancer—Patients—Religious life. 3. Consolation. 4. Death—Religious aspects—Christianity. 5. Christian biography. I. Waite, Don, 1950– II. Title.
BV4910.33.H55   2008
248.8'66092—dc22 [B]   2008006914

ISBN 978-0-8254-2899-9

Printed in the United States of America

08 09 10 11 12 / 5 4 3 2 1

Contents

Contents

Charlotte Hill

In loving memory of
Peter Hill

" ... to live is Christ and to die is gain."
Philippians 1:21

Jerry + Shirley,

Great to see you again.

Best wishes for God's continued
blessings.

Joyfully Yours,

Don Waite

Acknowledgments

THANKS to our spouses, Dave Hill and Ellie Waite. Your understanding, encouragement, and support kept us going. We love you!

Margaret Smith, dear friend and writer, your insight and guidance are very much appreciated.

And to our little sister, Sena Bergquist, we owe a huge debt of gratitude—your countless hours of pouring over our manuscript, editing and revising it, greatly improved our work. You believed in us when we were ready to call it quits. This book would not be here without your help.

Prologue

Peter's Story

THE phone rang on March 12, 1998, a cold Thursday evening. Peter, my youngest son, was calling from the McMinnville Hospital emergency room. A CAT scan had just revealed cancer in his liver. I'd prayed this call would never come, the call signaling Peter's imminent death.

～

While playing basketball in June of 1994, the contact lens Pete wore in his right eye ripped. Instantly, his view of the court became so blurred he couldn't continue playing, even though an eye examination the previous summer had reported 20/20 vision in his left eye. Wanting back on the court, he went to an ophthalmologist the following day for a replacement lens. To our shock, a tumor was found in his "good" eye. Within two weeks, a biopsy confirmed malignant ocular melanoma, a nearly unheard-of disease in a seventeen-year-old. Surgery was scheduled to remove his eye, abruptly ending Pete's involvement in summer basketball.

The crisis rocked our family. The loss of Pete's eye overwhelmed my husband, Dave. Fear that our son might die consumed me—a thought so abhorrent I refused to verbalize it. Head buried between his hands, our oldest son, Sam, cried, "Poor Pete. Poor Pete." Andy, our optimistic middle child, assured us everything would be okay, everything including Peter. Anxious to get the doctor stuff over with, Pete only wanted to put this episode behind him and go on with his life.

Before we could catch our breath, Pete's eye was extracted. Surgery went smoothly. In the recovery room, groggy from anesthesia, Pete slurred his words, his tongue hanging out of the corner of his mouth, drool dribbling down his chin. Still, he tried his hardest to smile and be polite to a nurse offering him something to drink. Dave and Andy doubled over with laughter at the goofy results. I glared at the two of them, whispering, "Stop it. You'll make him feel bad." That got Peter rolling. With a laugh and a lopsided grin, he enjoyed this brief respite with his dad and brother.

Later that day, the doctor's report momentarily relieved our fears—Pete's eye socket looked clear of melanoma. Then, the other shoe dropped. The doctor explained it would be twenty years before Peter could be considered out of the woods. If a single cancer cell penetrated his bloodstream, chance of survival was slim to none.

Released from the hospital, his eye socket still bandaged, Peter joined his brothers, cousins, and a few friends on our Christmas-tree farm, playing hide-and-seek. As they scattered in all directions to hide, a girl yelled at Pete, "You're it!" All of a sudden she realized he was the guy recently "disabled." She froze, horrified at what she'd blurted out. Pete looked at her and with a low chuckle responded, "Yeah, that's right, pick on the handicapped." The ice broken, everyone relaxed, and Pete was "it."

Two weeks after surgery, Peter was on the football field for pre-season practice. From outward appearances, his reduced range of vision and loss of depth perception left him unfazed. Toward the end of the season he confided his initial anxiety about playing with only one eye. Quietly, though, he'd given it his best shot. That season, his junior year, Seaside High School won the state championship in football, with Pete earning all-league and all-state honors.

Basketball proved a more difficult game with restricted vision. Pete's coach assumed he wouldn't play, but Pete said, "I've always played—it never occurred to me not to turn out." Forced to work harder on the court, Peter constantly pivoted his head and body in order to compensate for his blind side. When he missed a shot or a pass, he never used his impaired vision as an excuse. At the end of the season, Peter was chosen by his coaches and teammates as the most improved player, best defensive player, and most inspirational player.

During his senior year of football, Pete was called on during some games to play every down—offensively as running back, defensively as middle linebacker, as well as on special teams. Despite the extreme mental and physical strain, Pete gave what was asked. Coaches recognized his efforts, presenting him with the Iron Man and Most Coachable awards. Pete's respect of authority made a difference. Later, that attitude would carry through in dying as he gave himself to God—lock, stock, and barrel.

Track was the sport least affected by Pete's loss of an eye. In his senior year he usually posted one of the fastest, and often *the* fastest, 400-meter dash time in the state of Oregon for schools in Seaside's classification. After placing third at the state track meet his junior year, the two runners who beat him graduated, leaving Pete a realistic chance of becoming the state champ.

But during the district meet, while anchoring the short relay, he pulled his hamstring. With his leg wrapped, he attempted to run the open 400. From the starting blocks, pain crippled him. His best effort produced only an agonizing limp around the track. The coach yelled, "Hey, Pete. It's okay to stop." Yet Peter continued at a snail's pace. He finished his last high school race to a standing ovation, baffled to get acclamation for coming in dead last. Recognizing him as the fastest, some spectators cried. Losing his opportunity to win a state championship disappointed him; nevertheless, once it was over, it was over. Unlike his mother, he never talked about it with regret.

Taking rigorous academic courses, Peter achieved top grades. His history teacher said, "He thinks for himself. He wrestles with the issues before coming to a conclusion, then he voices well thought-out ideas, often contrary to popular opinion." One English instructor, believing Pete had the intellect, encouraged him to apply to Ivy League schools. The compliments that meant the most to Pete, though, were the ones that reflected his teachers' view of him as a genuinely nice guy, fun to have in class.

In June of 1996, Peter graduated with honors from Seaside High, receiving a number of awards, scholarships, and eleven varsity letters, as well as winning the affection and respect of his friends and teachers. A close friend of his told me Pete was a really easy guy to love, but Pete had also earned his respect, a commodity he did not freely give.

Instead of applying to an Ivy League school, Pete chose to stay closer to home. He started his college career as a history major at Linfield College, a small, private liberal arts school in McMinnville, Oregon. While excelling in the classroom, he joined the track team, but physical challenges again hindered him. His sore hamstring still bothered him, and a new injury caused painful swelling to his knee, slowing him down even more. Nonetheless, Pete ran, although his times were comparable to those clocked his sophomore year in high school. The summer after his freshman year, surgery repaired his damaged knee, leaving him determined to win some races.

That fall, Pete devoted himself to class work and conditioning, while still managing to find time for his buddies and his girlfriend, Amy. But when he came home at Christmas break, he didn't look well. His skin was pale, and he lacked his usual energy. Concerned, we made an appointment with a cancer specialist. The February checkup came back normal.

Yet, a nagging suspicion whispered that something was wrong. The Saturday before the emergency room call, Dave and I watched Pete compete in a track meet. After running, he looked gray and haggard. "I feel dead," he murmured, "just dead." Still, he ran his leg in the 1600-meter relay. Much later, we found out that Pete had been having pain in his side for several weeks before that meet.

Peter's Story

In the days following the competition, the pain became so bad he couldn't stand up straight or sleep. At that point, he talked to his coach. Pete was sent to the hospital, leading to the phone call we'd all dreaded.

After receiving the devastating news, Dave and I drove the hundred miles that night to bring him home. We stood in his dorm room, feeling uncomfortable and helpless, not knowing what to say, totally overwhelmed. No reassuring clichés could make things better. Normal conversation seemed out of place. Peter's best friend, Nick, and roommate, Dusty, quietly watched him pack. Nick, head bowed, fought tears. A feeling of oppression hung in the room, making breathing difficult for me. Nick and Dusty hugged Peter good-bye, the first of a miserably long series of heartbreaking farewells.

At Oregon Health and Science University (OHSU) Hospital a biopsy confirmed melanoma in his liver. The road would be much harder this time, making the ordeal with his eye seem like a jog on the track. Getting right in Peter's face for emphasis, his doctor stated, "You have got to understand that what you have is bad—very, very, very bad."

As Peter's doctor laid out medical options, one startled us—no treatment at all. Pete could go home and enjoy what little time remained. No remedy existed to cure him, no matter how desperately we wanted one. Grasping for a shred of hope, we found none. Wanting to buy him some time, we chose aggressive chemotherapy along with shots to stimulate his immune system.

A sense of unreality prevailed. For a few weeks, Peter stayed relatively active, although he felt much less energetic. He wanted to resume his schooling, but was told he'd be too sick once treatments began.

Dropping out of college crushed Peter. His future evaporated in the blink of an eye as he strove to come to terms with his mortality. Nothing would ever be the same. Dave and I took him to Linfield College's track one last time and waited in the car while Peter said good-bye to coaches and teammates. Plans for a better track season vanished. Knowing that his life was ending at the age of twenty exploded our world into a million pieces.

Sam, now married, and Andy, a teacher in Portland, came home to spend time with Pete. Hidden by the dining room curtains, through a veil of tears, I watched our three sons, laughing and roughhousing while playing basketball. Using their special names for each other and the offbeat slang spoken only when together, they savored their time as brothers. But Pete was dying. The happiness I normally felt at having the boys together was extinguished. My spirit weighed down with sorrow, I dreaded the future.

On the first Sunday after Peter came home with cancer, the congregation sang the hymn "All to Jesus I Surrender." The words stuck in my throat, knowing God was asking me to release Pete and trust him regardless of what tomorrow may bring.

My brother Don's almost daily phone calls and many letters to Pete reassured our family of Christ's faithfulness in our toughest times. Jesus hadn't and wouldn't abandon us. Even in death he would be there.

Although scared, Pete remained positive. "My life's been wonderful," he told me. "I'm fortunate to have a great family and friends I love." Fairness wasn't an issue. "Cancer happens," he calmly stated. "I'm no better than anyone else, so why not me?" Sadness, pain, and unanswered questions struggled within him, yet no bitterness.

Worried about his tight control of emotions, I said, "It's okay to cry, Pete."

With a sad little smile, he answered, "I have, Mom—at night, in bed." But I never saw his tears. My heart broke even more at the thought of Pete crying alone in the dark.

A tight-knit group of friends upheld Peter with calls, letters, and visits. Early in his illness, some of his Linfield College friends took off after class to see him. Laughing and talking, they spent the evening as they had when Pete was well. But he wasn't well, and the reality of death was hard to face.

Amy expressed her love for Pete in countless ways. Whenever possible, she stayed at his side, offering company and encouragement. Pete's suffering became hers, and the sharing of it drew them closer together. Their love grew, no matter how much it hurt.

Once treatment began, Pete's physical condition rapidly worsened. Horrible side effects from chemotherapy forced him to be hospitalized. Pete's blood counts dropped dramatically, requiring blood transfusions. Violent shakes plagued his body. Rashes from medication tormented him with itching. Secondary infections added to his misery. In a matter of weeks, he plummeted from a strong, graceful athlete to a weak, emaciated invalid.

Losing his strength bothered Pete terribly. Running miles had been his norm; now a short walk challenged his wasted body. "Don't think there's anything about this I like," he once informed me. That's as bad as his complaining ever got. After I read to him some Bible verses dealing with suffering producing character and earning eternal rewards, he asked me, "Do you really think I'm suffering?" Dave read him portions of the book of Job. Laughing, Pete retorted, "I don't have a thing to complain about."

Following two massive rounds of chemotherapy and bouts in the hospital, tests revealed cancer in his chest cavity. Nothing more could be done for him but to pray. And we prayed fervently.

June seventh, two days after Peter's twenty-first birthday, a severe frenzy of coughing caught him by surprise. Peter fought to breathe as Dave and I drove him to the emergency room. He was admitted to Seaside Hospital with double pneumonia. His condition quickly deteriorated.

A day later, Peter lay bedridden. Battling for every breath, he was able to get air only with the aid of an oxygen mask. His heart raced with the exertion of it, as if running a never-ending marathon. He was overcome with exhaustion, but his labored breathing wouldn't permit sleep or even rest. Conserving energy, he rarely spoke more than a couple of words at a time. Just breathing exacted every ounce of strength and self-control he possessed.

When asked by his doctor if he wanted to be put on a ventilator, Peter sought our opinions before making his decision. Dave and Andy encouraged him to grab hold of any available help, no matter how minute the hope. After being informed he would die on the machine, Sam and I worried about prolonging his suffering, not his life. Pete rejected the ventilator, saying, "It's time to live by faith."

During that last week, well-wishers frequently dropped in to visit Peter. His friends Nick, Sally, Barney, and Dusty came faithfully every day, staying for hours at a time. Because of Peter's breathing problems and his friends' sadness, conversation dwindled to a few scattered sentences. Yet Peter remained aware of their presence. At one point, worried about his friend sitting on the floor out of his sight, he croaked out, "Where's Sally?" Waving her hand above her head, Sally assured him, "I'm here, Peter. I'm right here."

Longing to demonstrate their love and concern, Sam and Andy stood on either side of Peter's bed and, while supporting his back, they tenderly bathed him with washcloths. Peter basked in his older brothers' attention.

Our pastor liked to end his visits with a song. Invariably, Pete picked "Amazing Grace." Family and friends surrounded Peter's bed, giving an emotional, if not melodious rendition of that wonderful old hymn, bringing him hope.

As the week progressed, a feeling of peace became apparent in Pete's room. His uncle, Don, perceived the Spirit of God at work and waited for something extraordinary to happen.

On the day Pete died, Jake, a buddy from track days, came to say good-bye. Sitting near the foot of Pete's bed, Jake left the room several times to gain control of his emotions. Aware of Jake's struggle, Pete moved his hand to get his attention. Even wiggling his fingers demanded a staggering effort for Pete's oxygen-starved body. As I watched from the doorway, Jake got up and held Pete's hand. No words were spoken, yet I felt how much Pete wanted to comfort his brokenhearted friend, to assure Jake he was fine.

Attending school in California, one of Pete's cousins and closest friends, Scott, found it vital to see Peter. Informed time was running out, he scrapped plans to drive home and caught the first available flight, arriving at the hospital the afternoon Pete died. With hands clasped, the two briefly visited and even laughed. As he walked by me, leaving Peter's room, Scott remarked, "I feel two hundred percent better. I know he's okay now."

Late that afternoon, a former teammate entered the room. He dropped a folded, battered team photo on Pete's stomach, and quickly fled without saying a word. In the hall, overcome with grief, his friend broke down in racking sobs. At Pete's memorial service, he told Dave the team picture meant the world to him, that being part of the championship team was the most important experience of his life. When discouraged, he'd almost quit, but Peter's encouragement kept him on the football field. He hadn't forgotten Pete's kindness.

Needing to preach the next morning, Don said his final goodbye hours before Pete died. Standing at the foot of his bed, Don reminded him of an earlier conversation. Months before, Don had promised to carry Pete in prayer, just as four determined men in the gospel of Mark carried their paralytic friend to Jesus for healing. "I'm still praying, Pete," Don said. "If you're too tired and weak to pray, don't worry. I'm still holding my end of your mat." Too exhausted to speak, Pete nodded his head, his face reflecting deep inner peace. In the hallway Sam and Don held each other and wept.

Around six that evening, Peter's sprint to the finish line began in earnest. His breathing, rapid and shallow, collapsed the oxygen mask, gluing it tightly to his face. His body writhed in an agonized effort to breathe, and his face contorted in pain. Pete was suffocating! Dave rushed to the nurse's station for help. Frantically, Sam strained to pry the mask loose in order to let air refill it.

A nurse cranked on the oxygen valve, slightly increasing the flow. For a brief moment, Peter seemed annoyed by the returning air. As he relaxed a bit, his breathing slowed but remained extremely labored. He lay quietly, eyes closed, his condition unchanged for several hours. Then, to our surprise, Pete began to speak. His voice was low, yet for the first time in days, he possessed the strength to talk conversationally. Mentally aware and lucid, his words conveyed God's love at work within him.

"God appeared to me when I was suffocating. Even when the oxygen mask collapsed as I fought for breath, God was right there. I wasn't afraid—total peace overcame me even when it looked awful to you. God promised Jesus would come for me soon."

Turning to his brother, he apologized. "Sorry about your wedding, Andy." Andy was counting on Peter to be his best man in his upcoming wedding. With Sam, the carpenter, Pete joked about the barn raising they'd have when celebrating their reunion in heaven. Giving fair warning to his cousin, Craig, Pete bragged, "I'll beat you in Ping-Pong next time we play. I'll have two eyes again." To his fishing buddies he promised, "Heaven's best fishing holes will be checked out before you get there."

A nurse came in and asked Pete if there was anything she could do to make him more comfortable. "No, I'm fine," he said. "I don't need a thing."

As Dave fussed with a wet washcloth on Pete's forehead, Peter gently told his dad to relax. "I am relaxed," Dave responded.

Pete challenged him, "Don't sweat the small stuff. Get the big picture."

Dave told Pete, "It seems I've been watching you compete in sports for a long time and I'm still at it. I hope you don't mind."

"Dad, I wouldn't have it any other way," he answered. "You're the best man I've ever known."

Constantly at Peter's side, Amy held his hand as she smiled at him, then dropped her head to his hand, saying, "You're the best thing to ever come into my life, and I love you very much. I'll never love anyone like I love you."

"No one but God," replied Peter.

As she smiled at Pete, he told her, "Seek God." Later, as Amy had her head down sobbing, Pete asked her to find comfort in Jesus. She kissed his cheek and put her head down again. Pete tugged her hand and said with a sweet smile, "Kiss me again."

I sat on the edge of his bed, my hand resting on his leg. Pete said, "I love you, Mom." I felt that love pour from him. More than anything, I wanted Pete to know how much I loved him, how proud he made me, how very much I would miss him.

With laughter, Pete, Sam, and Andy remembered the wonderful times they shared growing up, while tenderly expressing their love for each other in the present moment. Pete told his grandparents they were "the greatest." Each of the thirteen people crowded around his bed received individual words of love, hope, and peace. At some point Dave whispered, "It's okay to go, Pete."

Softly, he answered, "That's not my call to make, Dad. I'm waiting. Christ will return for me."

My sister, Betty, sat at the foot of Peter's bed. She later told me that the words from the hymn "Turn Your Eyes upon Jesus" had been running through her head.

Although we all reminisced with Peter about the past, our talk centered most on our anticipated reunion in heaven. With tremendous love and concern for those he would leave behind, Peter said good-bye. Continually, he brought our attention back to the Lord. "Find your comfort in Christ. God *is* good. God is *very* good. Christ is the answer." God's grace permeated the room, as the Spirit of God filled Pete. His last words to us were, "Don't worry about me. I love you all. I love everybody in this room. God bless you all. God bless you all."

Then he fell asleep.

An hour later, Peter awoke unmindful of the people surrounding him. He smiled, and then grinned as though seeing something extraordinary! Awestruck, his chin dropped to his chest. All the while, his eyes were intensely fixed on something above, something we couldn't see. Peter's eyebrows rose until his forehead crinkled in wonder. Then his eyes clamped shut as though blinded by a brilliant light. His face radiant, he exclaimed, "It's more beautiful than you can ever imagine!" Suddenly, he ripped off his oxygen mask. Miraculously, Pete breathed freely without assistance. Nodding his head up and down in response to someone, he shouted, *"Let's go! Let's go! Woo hoo! This is awesome! This is awesome! Yeah!"* Sitting straight up, he swung his arms and body back and forth as though flying from his bed. Dave tried to restrain him, but Pete's overpowering strength knocked him back. The force of his swinging arms dashed the IV stand and bedside tray against the wall and sent them crashing to the floor. That quiet corner of Seaside Hospital was rocked as Pete flew with wings of joy into the arms of Jesus.

Tears of sorrow and wonder mingled and flowed down our cheeks.

Peter is home.

1

Every Chapter Better
Than the One Before

BOOKS captivated Peter at an early age. As a toddler, he joined his older brothers for the nightly ritual of reading. Snuggled on Dave's or my lap, he was swept away in the marvelous adventures of Tom Sawyer, Peter Pan, and countless others. Spellbound, he hung on every word, crying when Old Yeller died or laughing hilariously at Jay Berry Lee's antics in *Summer of the Monkeys*.[1] But the most treasured of all the boys' childhood books were the Chronicles of Narnia, the seven-book series by C. S. Lewis; they were read, reread, and read again.

Narnia grew to be almost a part of Peter. One summer day, he and his brothers splashed and swam in the river that flows through our family homestead. Taking on the English accent of his Narnian friends, he playfully declared, "Mum, I'm having a jolly good time."

In grade school, Peter developed into a voracious reader. Even before he reached fourth grade, J. R. R. Tolkien's Lord of the Rings trilogy won his heart. Frodo, Samwise, Gandalf, and the other Rings characters became Pete's new friends. By high school, he practically had the books memorized. His sister-in-law, Justine, diligently searched the trilogy for obscure details, thinking she would stump him, but she never did. Looking toward graduate school, Pete contemplated doing a master's thesis on Tolkien's unpublished works.

When liver cancer forced Pete home, Dave and I received the gift of our "little boy" back for three priceless months. Too weak to read by himself, Dave and I read to Pete as we had done years before. Instead of cuddling on our laps, he now lay on the couch, looking out the window at the hills he loved. To my surprise, he rejected his beloved Tolkien books in preference for his boyhood favorites, choosing to hear either the Chronicles of Narnia or the Bible.

Narnia, the enchanted land of adventure, danger, good versus evil, and talking animals once again came alive and somehow seemed believable as Lewis spun his magical tales. Aslan, the great lion and Christ-figure in the book series, reinforced for Pete the realness of Christ. Facing untold perils, the Narnian children learn to trust Aslan as their only source of security, even when he is silent and seems far away.

The seventh Narnia book ends with remarkable images of heaven. Lewis's metaphor of death leading to life—just as the beginning pages of a favorite book start the adventure—caught Pete's imagination, helping him set his heart on the reality of spending eternity with his Lord:

> All their life in this world and all their adventures in Narnia had only been the cover and the title page: now at last they were beginning Chapter One of the Great Story which no one on earth has read: which goes on forever: in which every chapter is better than the one before.[2]

Onward to the prize before us!
Soon His beauty we'll behold;
Soon the pearly gates will open;
We shall tread the streets of gold.
—Eliza E. Hewitt,
"When We All Get to Heaven"

April 29, 1998

Dear Peter,

You're constantly in my thoughts and prayers. I recall the year you lost your eye but kept playing football, basketball, and running track. You inspired your teammates, and together you won the state championship in football. Your inner strength on and off the field affected many people, including me. But this time, the battle is much too big for you to handle alone, even with your remarkable courage. You will need to lean on God, "who is able to do immeasurably more than all we ask or imagine, according to his power that is at work within us" (Eph. 3:20). Believing divine power can defeat cancer, I keep committing you into God's care day by day, hour by hour, and sometimes moment by moment.

Pete, in the midst of your battle with cancer, I want you to experience more and more of Christ's love. He—not your medical diagnosis or prognosis—is the final truth. Medicine focuses on your body, knowing nothing about your soul, the meaning of suffering, love, life, or death. Only God can speak the truth of these matters to your heart.

Even as I pray for God to do a mighty miracle and heal you, I feel a need to talk to you about dying. Most people consider it a depressing topic and hesitate to bring it up. Yet the Bible frequently speaks of death. I mention it now, not because I think your cancer will inevitably end that way, but to encourage your faith.

Many believe the way to fight a terminal illness is to deny the possibility of death as if denial were an expression of faith. Their response reminds me of an ostrich burying its head in the sand. I have observed people die like this, denying death with their last breath, pretending their lack of acknowledgment will postpone it. Too often, those who take this approach die bitter, fearful, and lonely. The pain in their souls exceeds their physical suffering. Pete, I want something better for you. God's love is the antidote to this soul pain and fear.

There's a breed of horse called the Andalusian. These horses are used in Spain during bullfights. Unlike most horses, an Andalusian turns to face a threat instead of running from it. When an enemy chases an Andalusian, it instinctively pivots to confront the enemy. That is how God wants us to respond to our fears, including our fear of dying.

As a pastor, I've witnessed many people face death like Andalusians, replacing fear with genuine courage. This is not phony bravado but the natural result of facing life and death with faith in Christ. Millions of Christian martyrs have demonstrated this truth over the centuries. They lived well and they died well. They knew what the apostle Paul meant when he wrote, "For to me, to live is Christ and to die is gain" (Phil. 1:21). So continue to live like an Andalusian, ready to face death whenever it comes.

God is at work in you, Peter, therefore, "be strong in the Lord and in his mighty power" (Eph. 6:10). I suspect this time people will continue to be impressed by your strength and courage, but they will be even more impressed with the Lord's love and power at work in you. Look to him. Lean on him. Seek him always.

Hang in there, nephew! The Lord is on your side (see Rom. 8:31), and so am I.

Love,
Uncle Don

———

I can learn what it means to suffer with [Christ], sharing in his death, so that, somehow, I can experience the resurrection from the dead! . . . I am focusing all my energies on this one thing: Forgetting the past and looking forward to what lies ahead, I strain to reach the end of the race and receive the prize for which God, through Christ Jesus, is calling us up to heaven. (Phil. 3:10–11, 13–14 NLT)

2

Hamlet

HAMLET is a small valley nestled in the coastal mountains of northwest Oregon. Although secluded and, to some, lonely, Pete knew it as beautiful. The north fork of the Nehalem River flows through it, surrounded by a patchwork of forests and meadows. In the late 1800s, Peter's great-grandfather, a Finnish immigrant, homesteaded the property we call home.

Peter was born and raised in this peaceful valley, and Hamlet held a special place in his heart. A country boy, he deeply appreciated God's creation. Wildflowers and trickling waterfalls—as well as deer, elk, eagles, and other wildlife that abound in this area—proclaimed God's majesty and love to him. Standing on our front porch and listening to the wind blow in the treetops stirred his spirit.

Five and six years younger than his brothers, Pete followed Andy and Sam into the forest from the time he was a preschooler. As he grew older, the three of them would spend hours hiking and exploring the steep hills behind our house. They particularly enjoyed one trek that took them miles away, to a high clear-cut with a spectacular view of Mount Hood. Hunting and fishing added to their time outdoors.

Often my husband, Dave, and our boys spent the day building lean-tos in the woods. With twine, tree limbs, and a plastic tarp, they'd erect a crude shelter that fostered happy memories. Dave taught survival skills and imparted his lifelong knowledge of the forest. Clustered around the mandatory campfire, Peter forged close bonds with his family and the land we occupy.

The week Pete came home with liver cancer, Craig, his good friend and cousin, journeyed with Peter for miles over the logging roads and trails that lace Hamlet. After Pete died, we received a letter from Craig, which described Pete's last physically active day before cancer robbed him of strength. Craig wrote,

> I wonder if Pete ever told you about the day we drove the fat cats [motorcycles]. That was the single greatest day of my life. . . . My memory is so clear; it's almost as if I placed a video in the VCR and am watching the day replayed.
>
> We traveled to Antilla Falls, parked the bikes, and walked to the fish ladder. The river was incredibly high and fast flowing. Crossing the footbridge, we sat on the concrete wall just above the waterfall, our feet almost touching the water as we talked.
>
> I told Pete I had heard of another waterfall almost forty feet tall somewhere in Hamlet. Pete thought he and Andy had been there once before, but he couldn't remember exactly where, yet believed he could find it. We rode to the washout, and then hiked into the woods in search of the falls. After a while, we heard water crashing down on rocks.
>
> Following the sound, we slashed our way through the thick brush. Without a trail, we let the roar of the falls beckon us farther. Sliding down a steep slope, we finally arrived. It was breathtaking. Mountains of water tumbled down the falls, sounding like rolling thunder striking the rocks. Pete and I discovered this wonderful place, and sat absorbing the beauty. Everything seemed perfect . . .
>
> After we had our fill of the waterfall, Pete wanted to ride to a spot that overlooks your property. We found it and

again sat and talked. I remember looking over at his face as he surveyed the panoramic view of your house and tree farm. Wistfully, Pete smiled. I think he wanted to cry.

Letting go of the land that he so loved hurt Peter deeply. Yet minutes before he died, seeing what we couldn't see, he exclaimed in wonder, "It's more beautiful than you can ever imagine!" The land Pete cherished faded to a dim reflection of the unimaginably beautiful country he was about to enter. God called him to a world that is better by far.

~

> Fair are the meadows,
> Fairer still the woodlands,
> Robed in the blooming garb of spring.
> Jesus is fairer, Jesus is purer,
> Who makes the woeful heart to sing.
> —Joseph A. Seiss, translator
> "Fairest Lord Jesus"

April 30, 1998

Hi Pete,

As I sit by my study window, writing, I can see Mount Rainier glistening in the warm sunshine. Tulips are blooming, and spring is at its finest. The beauty overwhelms my senses.

I'm sure the view from your hospital room is much different. But maybe you, in a room filled with suffering, can appreciate the most glorious of all God's gifts better than I—the truth that God loves you with a love so immeasurably vast that he sent his Son to suffer and die for you. An old hymn captures this sense of astonishment: "Amazing love! How can it be, that Thou, my God, shouldst die for me?"[1]

Jesus could have stayed in heaven and avoided the cross, but instead he gave his life for us. Such love is almost inconceivable, pointing us to the knowledge that death is the door leading to eternity with Christ. It's why Paul could write in Philippians, "For to me, to live is Christ and to die is gain" (Phil. 1:21), and not have it be nonsense. Heaven seemed like a wonderful improvement to Paul, because he had already discovered that knowing Christ was the best thing life offered. Such a view wasn't wishful thinking but the natural consequence of receiving the love of Christ.

Paul so anticipated spending eternity with Jesus, he viewed death as gain. His deepest desire and need was for more of Jesus. With similar anticipation, your Aunt Ellie and I became engaged because we loved being together so much we wanted to spend the rest of our lives together. I couldn't wait to marry her! A few friends thought I was crazy, wanting to exchange my singleness for marriage. Having never experienced a relationship like ours, they looked at marriage with a sense of trepidation. Still, I viewed being married to Ellie as gain.

Peter, let cancer remind you of your greatest need: Jesus. As your awareness of your need grows, your desire for him will deepen. You will long to grow closer to him. This is what living for Christ means—it also prepares you to die well, since death brings you into a more intimate relationship with Jesus.

Peter, I am praying you will experience more of Jesus' love, even in the midst of your treatments and pain. He'll meet you where you're at. Then if you are healed, you can live a fuller, more purposeful life. But if not, you can die with peace and anticipation, knowing you will be with Jesus for all eternity. Trust him like a child. Ask him to hold you in his arms and carry you. I'm praying that for you.

Resting in Christ's love,
Uncle Don

May you have the power to understand, as all God's people should, how wide, how long, how high, and how deep his love really is. May you experience the love of Christ, though it is so great you will never fully understand it. Then you will be filled with the fullness of life and power that comes from God. (Eph. 3:18–19 NLT)

3

Father and Son

DURING the boys' growing-up years, Dave whiled away many evenings in their room, happy just to be close to them. Starting on the night Peter called from McMinnville Hospital and informed us of his illness, Dave quit work, freeing himself to be available for his dying son.

The Monday following Pete's return home from Linfield College, Dave and Pete hiked up and down the steep hillsides behind our house, an activity they had often shared in the past. They explored side streams and the little rivulets and waterfalls that Peter found fascinating, halting to appreciate the early spring wildflowers. Elk and deer flitted in and out of view as father and son traversed the countryside.

Stopping for lunch at the bottom of Little Creek Canyon, Pete surprised Dave by saying, "I'm not hungry, Dad, eat without me." Dave finished his peanut butter sandwich and apple before they attempted the climb up the near vertical bank leading out of the canyon. Slipping on a log, Pete fell, frightening Dave by saying, "I don't think I can make it out, Dad, I'm just too tired." Dave tried to make light of the situation by assuring Peter, "Sit and rest a bit; you'll soon be fine." A slow, tortuous ascent eventually brought them home.

That evening Dave confessed, "Char, I'm scared. Normally Pete dances circles around me on a hike like we took." Our eyes were opened to the gravity of Pete's condition. After that, when I looked at Dave, I saw pain etched on his face.

Hikes were soon out of the question. So Dave took Pete on pickup truck rides to get him outdoors. Finally the day came when Pete sadly said, "Let's stay put, Dad. I don't have what it takes for any more rides."

Finding themselves housebound, weather permitting, father and son enjoyed sitting together on the front porch, drinking coffee and appraising the hills they both loved. That ended when Pete's energy failed even to get him off the couch. Then, Dave sat indoors with him by the hour, frequently reading aloud Pete's favorite C. S. Lewis books.

Peter never faced a doctor's appointment, chemotherapy treatment, hospital stay, or medical procedure without his dad by his side. In his last week of life, Dave salvaged Pete's dignity. Bedridden, Pete couldn't handle his bathroom needs. Instead of depending on nurses, Dave willingly dealt with bedpans, his love unfailing.

Now, as usual, Dave finds comfort in God's creation. Like Pete, he draws strength from listening to God sing in the wind blowing through the treetops. When we walk in the woods, he often stops, kneeling down to point out a patch of wildflowers or small cluster of waterfalls and quietly comments, "Pete loved these." Invariably we pause to examine them. A little farther down the path he'll remember, "This is where we built a lean-to and spent the day playing." Or, "Pete and I planted this bunch of trees." And, "We sat here and watched a herd of elk." Memories of Pete are everywhere.

Our conversations usually end on a note like this: "What's Pete seeing now?" Dave thinks of the day he'll witness new sights with his son. Pete promised he'll have a few special places handpicked to share on that longed-for day. We have an eternity of marvelous adventures waiting for us.

Father and Son

There's a land that is fairer than day,
And by faith we can see it afar;
For the Father waits over the way
To prepare us a dwelling place there.

In the sweet by and by,
We shall meet on that beautiful shore;
In the sweet by and by,
We shall meet on that beautiful shore.
—Sanford F. Bennett,
"In the Sweet By and By"

May 1, 1998

Dear Peter,

I wish we were together hiking the woods at Hamlet on a beautiful day like this. I treasure my two summers working in the forest there with your dad. Compared to the freedom of roaming those hills, I can only imagine how confining a hospital room feels. Add chemo, and your misery must be off the charts.

Cancer has robbed you of so many things you love. Yet you never complain. First, you lost your eye. More recently, you had to give up your spring semester at Linfield College. You've probably forgotten what it's like to simply feel good, to live a day without pain.

But maybe there's something to learn from all this pain. The apostle Paul learned from his suffering and deprivation. He was beaten and imprisoned, shipwrecked, rejected and hated because of his commitment to Jesus. His difficulties changed his outlook in surprising ways. He came to consider the things he lost to be of no more value than garbage, compared with what really mattered. "I have lost all things," Paul said, "[but] I consider them rubbish, that I may gain Christ" (Phil. 3:8).

Jesus wants to overturn our perspectives on gain and loss: "Anyone who intends to come with me has to let me lead. You're not in the driver's seat—I am. Don't run from suffering; embrace it. Follow me and I'll show you how" (Luke 9:23 MSG).

Paul says the same thing a little differently: "I have died, but Christ lives in me. And I now live by faith in the Son of God, who loved me and gave his life for me" (Gal. 2:20 CEV). The Bible says that to live—really live—you must die to the things of this world, releasing things of secondary importance to discover what really counts. "For to me, to live is Christ and to die is gain" (Phil. 1:21). You and I must let go of other things, even the good things, in order to fully live for him. Then we can discover what we gain through Christ: assurance of his love, acceptance, and an understanding of what really matters—an enduring confidence in eternal life.

Peter, I know you trust in Christ, and he is showing you these truths in a deeper way than I could ever articulate. He will transform your losses into gains, as your trust grows. Whatever you lose, you still have him, and he has you. I continue to commit you into his loving care every day.

I love you,
Uncle Don

As surely as we died with Christ, we believe we will also live with him. We know that death no longer has any power over Christ. He died and was raised to life, never again to die. (Rom. 6:8–9 CEV)

4

The News

THE night we learned Pete's cancer had returned, our family was hurled into a bottomless pit: hope seemed to die with the news.

Earlier that day I'd headed home from work, nothing more pressing on my mind than what to fix for dinner. Reading was on the agenda for the rest of the evening, like hundreds of evenings before. But Dave met me as I came through the back door. "Peter called from McMinnville Hospital," he said. "The emergency room doctor thinks he may have appendicitis. They're waiting for test results." My reaction frightened me—*Pete doesn't have appendicitis, he has cancer.* I knew it. I felt it, even as I hoped it wasn't so.

Anxiously, we waited for further word from Peter. Unsettled and scared, I longed for relief from the tension tying me into knots. Tears were preferable to the emptiness I experienced, yet they didn't come. An eternity later, the phone rang. Fearing the news, part of me didn't want to answer.

"Mom, my cancer's back," Peter's flat, emotionless voice reported. "A CAT scan shows tumors throughout my liver and abdomen."

"No, Pete. No," I softly cried. Then unthinkingly, "You've got to be kidding," tumbled from my mouth.

He answered, "I wouldn't joke about this."

"Of course not, I'm sorry," I responded. And I was so terribly sorry about everything.

As we drove to McMinnville to bring Peter home that awful

night, silence enveloped the car—both Dave and I absorbed in our private thoughts. Our hearts fought the fear we couldn't voice: "We're losing Pete."

Near silence continued in Pete's dorm room. Avoiding the subject dominating our thoughts, we concentrated on packing the first load of Pete's belongings. Around 9:30 we set out for Hamlet.

Hungry, we stopped for a burger on our way out of town. *This is weird,* I remember feeling. *Peter is dying—and here we are bothering with such mundane matters as eating.*

Later that night, the daunting task confronted me—passing the horrible news to relatives. Sena, my youngest sister, topped my list. She answered her phone and immediately knew something dreadful had occurred. Unintelligible groans escaped my throat as I struggled to force out, "Pete has liver cancer." After much repeating on my part, Sena eventually understood. I was relieved and thankful when she offered to contact the rest of the family.

So the news was spread. The beginning of the end started. Yet upon reflection, I can trace God's leading through it all. God transformed the bad news to good . . . the ugly to beautiful . . . the weak to strong . . . the imperfect to perfect. Hope hadn't died, but sprang forth stronger than ever.

⌒

Oh! sometimes the shadows are deep,
And rough seems the path to the goal,
And sorrows, sometimes how they sweep
Like tempests down over the soul.

O then to the Rock let me fly,
To the Rock that is higher than I
O then to the Rock let me fly
To the Rock that is higher than I!
—Erastus Johnson,
"The Rock That Is Higher Than I"

May 3, 1998

Dear Peter,

I hope this letter finds you on a good day, feeling few side effects from your treatments. For my part, I'm still smarting from an incident at church yesterday. Someone left an anonymous note criticizing my preaching. The censure seemed unfair and, quite frankly, made me mad. It also got me thinking about what you might be feeling.

Your situation makes my complaint seem trivial, especially since you've done nothing to deserve cancer. According to your mom you haven't gotten upset, but our family is pretty good at denying anger. Yet during a life-threatening illness, anger can spill out unexpectedly like a subscription card falling from a magazine.

The Bible records the anger of a righteous man suffering almost beyond endurance. Job had lost everything—his ten children were killed and his wealth disappeared in an instant. Covered in boils, berated by his wife and friends, Job became angry because he felt God had abandoned him during his time of greatest need.

David, Jeremiah, and even Jesus complained or protested when they could not find God's love, presence, or justice in the midst of their suffering. Jeremiah is called the weeping prophet. David filled the Psalms with his tormented and angry "laments" to God.

Jesus' agonizing cry from the cross, "My God, my God, why have you forsaken me?" (Matt. 27:46) erupted from the depths of his soul. His lament was not so much about physical pain, but his sense of losing the Father's love and companionship. He felt forsaken, betrayed, and alone.

The Psalms of lament (with one exception) reveal an interesting pattern: they begin in anger but are transformed into praise at the end. I believe God, even though he may not have changed the writers' circumstances, responded to their disappointment and anger by manifesting his presence. That's what happened to Job; in the end he discovered God was with him—and that's really all he needed.

Pete, if our heroes of faith cried out in anger, disappointment, or protest, then it's okay for you to do it, too. Laments, sometimes uttered through tears and groans, refuse to let go of God even when it feels as if God has let go of you. God is not offended by such honesty, but recognizes it as an expression of faith. God can handle your anger. Don't let it simmer. It will make you more miserable than the side effects of chemotherapy.

By being open with your anger, you may discover a merciful God who wins your heart and holds you close in loving arms. It can become the pathway to deeper intimacy with your Savior, a way of saying, "For to me, to live is Christ and to die is gain" (Phil. 1:21). Believe it. Do it. Let anger draw you closer to God.

Lamenting your suffering,
Uncle Don

My God, my God, why have you forsaken me?
  Why are you so far from saving me,
  so far from the words of my groaning?
O my God, I cry out by day, but you do not answer,
  by night, and am not silent.

(Ps. 22:1–2)

5

Home with Pete

JOY that he lived—and deep, heartbreaking sorrow that he was dying—accompanied Peter when he came home. On the surface, our life took on a pretense of normalcy. But underneath, all had radically changed, giving day-to-day encounters an aching poignancy. Knowing that time with him would soon end made every minute precious, yet so fleeting, increasing Pete's immeasurable worth to us. I wanted the clock turned back, making things as they were when Peter was home and well.

My heart broke with the bittersweetness of our being together, realizing my youngest would soon be gone. Seeing my agony, Peter would put his arms around me, saying, "Mom, I don't want to hurt you." Not wishing to add to his burden, I'd answer, "Don't worry about me, Pete, I'll be fine." At the time, I didn't know if I really believed I would ever be okay again. His kindness pierced me, causing me to more fully love and appreciate the son I was losing.

Lying in his usual place on the couch, looking out the window, Pete often kept his thoughts to himself, in many ways leaving me to guess what anguish he suffered. Yet he remained calm and pleasant. Even when quiet, he wasn't withdrawn, always desiring our company. Being with him made me feel better. At the same time it weighed me down, because I knew that soon he'd depart this world for good, taking part of me with him.

On his last day home, we celebrated his twenty-first birthday.

Pete hadn't the strength for opening presents and partying on the actual date, but two days later he rallied for the occasion. Watching him laughing and enjoying our family and Amy, I allowed myself to forget for a while the seriousness of his illness. Having fun, he drew us into his spirit of gaiety. Still, the reality of his condition wasn't buried deeply. The absence of the words "and many more," traditionally sung at the end of "Happy Birthday" in our family, spoke volumes, dampening the party atmosphere. Early in the evening, the birthday wrappings still littering the living room floor, we rushed Peter to the hospital with a sudden attack of breathing difficulties. He never came home again.

And "he never came home again" would be unbearable if that was the end of the story, but it isn't. Peter is truly home, the place he was created for. I find tremendous solace in that truth. As Dave said, "Pete's with his real Daddy now." I miss him; he has left an ache in my heart. But I know this—I'm also on the road home.

⌐

When peace, like a river, attendeth my way,
When sorrows like sea billows roll;
Whatever my lot, Thou has taught me to say,
It is well, it is well, with my soul.
                              —Horatio G. Spafford,
                              "It Is Well with My Soul"

May 5, 1998

Dear Pete,

I enjoyed talking with you last night and am praying you're able to go home from the hospital today. Chemo is a formidable foe. Your struggle with cancer reminds me of the story of Joshua. God raised up Joshua to lead his people into the land he had promised. Before his promise could be fulfilled, though, the Israelites had to defeat several strong armies. So it is with us. God's promises are not automatic; they require us to fight with faith, trusting him with the outcome.

The Lord told Joshua, "Be strong and courageous" (Josh. 1:6). Pete, this is also God's word to you. Your struggle, like Joshua's, requires much more than physical might. Spiritual courage and the strength that comes from trusting God are needed. Since we cannot win life's battles on our own, the Bible calls all Christians to "be strong in the Lord and in his mighty power" (Eph. 6:10).

The apostle Paul faced many life and death situations. Once, when his courage and strength wavered, God reassured him with these words: "My grace is sufficient for you, for my power is made perfect in weakness" (2 Cor. 12:9). Hold on to this promise, Pete, since none of us has what it takes to defeat cancer alone. Recognizing limitations, coming to the end of our own strength, activates God's power and teaches reliance upon Christ and his strength.

People who feel the need to be in charge seldom find

serenity while fighting a life-threatening disease. Maintaining constant vigilance, they cannot rest for even a moment. Worry and fear override any sense of peace. I have witnessed several Christians face serious illness with great determination but without quietness of heart. They thought it was up to them to defeat the disease, just as they believed they were responsible for overcoming every previous obstacle in life. Accepting death as beyond their control seemed intolerable to them. Their last days were filled with anxiety, anger, and frustration.

Peter, as you confront the possibility of dying, you will wrestle not only with cancer, but also with trust. Can you depend upon Jesus when your life is on the line? If the answer is yes, you will discover "the peace of God, which transcends all understanding" (Phil. 4:7) and his power which "is made perfect in weakness" (2 Cor. 12:9). Surrendering control is the key to dying well, just as it is to living well.

So, trust him, nephew. Let his peace fill you. Then you will be victorious, whatever the outcome. Remember our verse: "For to me, to live is Christ and to die is gain" (Phil. 1:21).

With love,
Uncle Don

—

Don't worry about anything; instead, pray about everything. Tell God what you need, and thank him for all he has done. If you do this, you will experience God's peace, which is far more wonderful than the human mind can understand. His peace will guard your hearts and minds as you live in Christ Jesus. (Phil. 4:6–7 NLT)

6

Acceptance

THE week following Pete's diagnosis of terminal cancer he said, "Mom, I don't know how to die; I've never done it before. I'm a fighter. I'm competitive by nature, but I don't want to fight God." This was not only a plea for help but also his first step in accepting the unthinkable: he was dying.

Peter referred to an inward, spiritual battle. It never occurred to him at this early stage in his illness not to pursue medical treatment. Doctors offered no cure, but the hopelessness of his condition was yet to soak in.

Pete's physician decided to throw everything at him, including the kitchen sink, saying, "Peter's young and incredibly strong. He can tolerate more chemo than many could survive." This began an extremely punishing regimen of chemotherapy. He opened the chemo room as the first patient of the day, and many hours later ended the day as the last patient out the door. The effects on his body were brutal, yet Pete consented to another bout, hoping for a miraculous cure or at least extended time.

Despite the two heavy rounds of chemotherapy, cancer filled Peter's chest cavity, lining his esophagus, aorta, bronchi, and alveoli. Doctors informed us that the last available option would require him being admitted to a critical care unit, hooked up to life support systems and administered interferon intravenously, bringing him close to the point of death before doctors unplugged the IV at the last possible moment. This drastic treatment could kill him, yet it held a remote hope of giving Pete a few more weeks, months at best.

After thinking it over, Peter made up his mind. "I won't go through anything so torturous without the chance of being cured," he said. "More time isn't enough."

To his relief, I replied, "I don't want you to undergo more suffering due to treatments, Pete." His decision brought him another step closer to total acceptance.

While coming to terms with the approach of his death, Peter continued living in anticipation of what he could still accomplish, never throwing in the towel or despairing. He planned on recovering from chemo enough to make firewood during the summer and then return to Linfield College in the fall.

Pete's post-chemo plans didn't work out, though. Instead of growing stronger, he grew weaker at an alarming rate. His resolve not to wrestle with God remained firm. Peter associated fighting God with a visit we'd had with friends. The couple's little boy, Norbert, painstakingly built a sand castle on the beach, then threw a temper tantrum when the tide came in, washing away his hard work. On hands and knees, Norbert screamed and railed as he frantically tried to push back the ocean with his arms, loudly demanding that the sea be stopped. Peter told me, "I don't want to be a Norbert, engaged in a war I can't win, shaking my fists at God." Instead, Pete chose to trust God, enabling him to face his pending death with courage and peace and, ultimately, joy.

On his deathbed, enveloped in God's love, Peter not only accepted but embraced death as the door to everlasting life with Christ. At just the right moment, his earthly journey finished, Pete soared through heaven's gates, joy-filled, powerful, and free.

⌁

O Joy that seekest me through pain,
I cannot close my heart to thee;

I trace the rainbow through the rain,
And feel the promise is not vain,
That morn shall tearless be.
　　　　　　—George Matheson,
　　"O Love That Wilt Not Let Me Go"

May 6, 1998

Hi Pete,

You were on my mind while I was playing a round of golf today at the local course. A doe and her fawn walked alongside the fairway, bringing back memories of when you and I played together at the Seaside course and saw the deer there. In the future, I hope we'll play again. Maybe we'll have a tournament at our next family reunion.

Pete, have you ever heard of Paul Azinger, a professional golfer on the PGA tour? Making over a million dollars a year doing what he loved, Azinger was living his dream. He seemed to have it all, until three words changed the course of his life, as they did yours, "You have cancer."

While he was reeling from that sobering news, someone shared this truth with him: "We think we are in the land of the living and headed for the land of the dying, when in reality we are in the land of the dying and headed for the land of the living."[1] If this were true, Azinger realized, it would change all of his assumptions, overturning everything he thought he knew.

We are now living in the land of the dying. I think that's what David tells us in Psalms: "Even though I walk through the valley of the shadow of death, I will fear no evil, for you are with me" (Ps. 23:4).

Our entire lives can be described as a journey through the valley of the shadow of death. This ominous shadow has often fallen across our paths: Grandpa and Grandma

Waite's deaths, your frequent cancer screenings, and your awareness that melanoma could reappear at any time. Every step of our journey brings us closer to our own deaths. But most of us don't acknowledge we are now in the land of the dying. It's just too depressing to face, unless we recognize the second part of the statement is also true: we are headed for the land of the living.

Ecclesiastes says we are made for eternity: "God has . . . planted eternity in the human heart" (Eccl. 3:11 NLT). Something deep inside us longs for a place where there is no death. God gave the apostle John a vision of the land of the living, which is described in Revelation:

> Now the dwelling of God is with men, and he will live with them. They will be his people, and God himself will be with them and be their God. He will wipe every tear from their eyes. There will be no more death or mourning or crying or pain, for the old order of things has passed away. (21:3-4)

It's where those who trust in Jesus are headed, a place where they will be with God and where death will no longer intrude. No one will grieve or ever cry in pain again.

Pete, this is the place Jesus has promised to take you. He said in the gospel of John, "When everything is ready, I will come and get you, so that you will always be with me where I am" (John 14:3 NLT). The Bible encourages you to see yourself as a sojourner and alien while passing through this land of the dying. You are just a temporary resident here. Heaven is your real home. You can trust Jesus with your very life. When the time is right, he will come for you.

May God fill both of our hearts with a desire for our real home: heaven. In the meantime, let's live for Christ, knowing that to die is gain.

Love,
Uncle Don

———

All these faithful ones died without receiving what God had promised them, but they saw it all from a distance and welcomed the promises of God. They agreed that they were no more than foreigners and nomads here on earth. And obviously people who talk like that are looking forward to a country they can call their own. If they had meant the country they came from, they would have found a way to go back. But they were looking for a better place, a heavenly homeland. That is why God is not ashamed to be called their God, for he has prepared a heavenly city for them. (Heb. 11:13–16 NLT)

7

The Pain of Loving

AMY faithfully and tenderly loved Peter. No matter how painful the journey, she walked each step with him, every fiber of her being hoping for a miracle.

When cancer involuntarily ended Pete's college career, Amy wanted to quit school in order to be with him. But with his encouragement, she remained at Oregon State University, spending many hours on the road driving to and from visiting him. While hospitalized in Portland, he counted on Amy to brighten his dreary existence. After classes, she'd hop in her car and travel to OHSU, returning to her apartment late at night, only to repeat the cycle the next day.

If Pete was home, Amy made the trip from Corvallis to Hamlet every weekend. Invariably, they took walks. From our family room window, I looked down to the road below. Hand in hand, they slowly moseyed along, stopping frequently for rest breaks. Even from a distance her concern for him showed. She'd lean into him as if to take some of his weight upon herself, treasuring their brief time alone.

Forced to hang out at home, Amy and Pete found pleasure in small things. I'd be working in the kitchen and call them to come see the family of baby rabbits residing in our back yard. They'd always enjoy a chuckle at the round, cuddly balls of brown fur and have a few comments to make: "What cute little bush bunnies. Look at the sweet little stars on their foreheads."

The Pain of Loving

They were comfortable with each other—their conversation and laughter came easily. Yet when Pete's illness put a damper on idle chitchat—it didn't seem to matter. For them, just being together was enough. Holding hands on the couch, Amy's head on his shoulder, the whisper of an occasional soft voice, quiet love filled the room.

During Pete's last week in Seaside Hospital, Amy sat by his side for hours on end. Sleep, food, and personal comfort took a back seat—her entire reason for living was to will Pete on. When he reacted to a medication with hallucinations and extreme agitation, Amy was there. Replacing his oxygen mask after he repeatedly knocked it off, trying to restrain his flailing arms, talking calmly to him—Amy did what she could. Up to the end her steadfast love and devotion never wavered.

Pete's death devastated Amy. She had dreamed of having the rest of the summer with Pete, of having time for walks on the beach. Time to figure things out. Time to talk. Time to love. And if necessary time to say good-bye. But more than anything, she had dreamed of spending her life with Peter.

Amy expressed her grief in the following lament.

epilogue

in the end
silence will cover the rough edges of sound

stillness will follow
drops of rain will melt on a black nylon umbrella
as the sky starts to fall

i can count the times i heard you say my name
somehow i can't forget how even my name can
sound like music when it falls like water and
rides on your tongue

51

you have left your fingerprints on my heart and i
will love you as long as i breathe
i am a glass half full of hope
half empty of you

i will wait for you
at the end of a long day
i won't turn the corner to see if you are coming
i will listen for the sound of my name on your lips
and close my eyes.

The half empty glass will someday overflow with the joy of their being together in heaven. Amy will turn the corner, see his face, and hear her name. Some bright and beautiful day.

⌒

Be still, my soul: the hour is hastening on
When we shall be forever with the Lord.
When disappointment, grief and fear are gone,
Sorrow forgot, love's purest joys restored.
Be still, my soul: when change and tears are past,
All safe and blessed we shall meet at last.
—Katharina A. von Schlegel,
"Be Still, My Soul"

May 8, 1998

Hi Pete,

It's a cool, overcast morning, and I am not highly motivated to get going. This type of morning makes me want to sit down with the sports page and a cup of coffee. However, my number-one priority is to spend a few minutes with you via this letter.

My frustration in writing these letters is that they are monologues. You hear lots from me, but I'm not able to hear your thoughts, questions, or insights. Have you heard God speaking to you or sensed his presence? How do you deal with your pain and suffering? Your mother tells me you never complain. She has never heard you ask, "Why me?"

Personally, I'm a weenie when it comes to pain. I remember breaking my hand while working with your dad. I was cranking a winch when the handle slipped, spun around, and smashed my hand several times. Compared to the anguish you're experiencing, my pain was minor.

My natural inclination is to see nothing positive about pain or suffering, but the Bible says they're God's tools to transform our character, making us more like Jesus. To paraphrase C. S. Lewis, pain is God's megaphone.[1] It gets our attention. James talks about suffering this way: "Whenever trouble comes your way, let it be an opportunity for joy. For when your faith is tested, your endurance has a chance to grow. So let it grow, for when your endurance is fully developed, you will be strong in character and ready for anything" (James 1:2-4 NLT).

Your Grandpa Waite's dad died when Grandpa was an infant, forcing his mother to give him up for adoption. When he was seven, his adopted mother died. After her death, he bounced between families until he struck out on his own at fourteen. He survived the depression and emerged a strong and principled family man. Character is not formed in the classroom or by some self-help technique. Character is forged through suffering.

Maybe that's one of the reasons God leaves us in this "land of the dying" as long as he does. The New Testament says, "Don't be surprised at the fiery trials you are going through, as if something strange were happening to you. Instead, be very glad—because these trials will make you partners with Christ in his suffering, and afterward you will have the wonderful joy of sharing his glory when it is displayed to all the world" (1 Peter 4:12-13 NLT).

God uses suffering to draw us closer to him, while at the same time teaching us to pray, to persevere, and to rely on him. In the midst of suffering we are presented with the opportunity to encounter Jesus in a deeper way than ever before. Or as I have heard, you will never know God is all you need until God is all you have.

Pete, I am not saying that God caused your suffering. Christians have debated the cause of suffering for centuries. But whatever the cause, God can redeem it. Only God can take something evil and ugly like cancer and create something good and beautiful from it when we respond in faith. I have seen it happen. So I urge you to pray not only for your suffering to end, but also that God will redeem it, using it to develop the character of Christ in you. And as this happens, you may one day find your cancer has become an opportunity for joy, because for us "to live is Christ and to die is gain" (Phil. 1:21). Hang in there, Peter. Your suffering has purpose.

Love,
Uncle Don

For his Holy Spirit speaks to us deep in our hearts and tells us that we are God's children. And since we are his children, we will share his treasures—for everything God gives to his Son, Christ, is ours, too. But if we are to share his glory, we must also share his suffering. Yet what we suffer now is nothing compared to the glory he will give us later. (Rom. 8:16–18 NLT)

8

Sam

BEING Peter's big brother was a job Sam took seriously. Before Pete's birth, it was five-year-old Sam who suggested Peter as the name for our expected baby. Since then, Sam's held the older brother's position as helper and protector, while Pete grew up admiring his big brother.

When Peter was a toddler, Sam asked, "What color is Peter's hair?"

"Brown," I replied.

Indignant that such a mundane word described his youngest brother, Sam retorted, "No, his hair is golden; it's beautiful. I wish my hair was that color." Implied criticism of Pete wasn't tolerated.

Shaken when cancer struck Peter, Sam's love and concern flowed through his actions. The summer Pete's eye was removed, Sam often became Peter's chauffeur, driving him to town or football practice. Engaged at the time, Sam even included Pete on his movie dates with his fiancée, Justine. She joined Sam in supporting Pete.

Three years and nine months later, when cancer invaded Pete's liver, Sam maintained his desire to help and protect his brother. He fervently wanted to donate his blood to ensure Pete received uncontaminated transfusions. He also hoped it might be a closer match, and Peter's body wouldn't react negatively to it. Sam was deeply disappointed that hospital procedure didn't allow this.

Sam was the one who drove Pete and his dad to Portland when

Peter got his first interleukin-2 and interferon shots in hope of stimulating his immune system. Amy and Andy met them at the hospital. After the shots, they all went to a Red Robin restaurant for lunch. While eating, flu-like symptoms with violent shakes hit Pete. Forgetting food, Sam bundled Pete back into the car, turned the heater on full force, trying to warm him up, and then sweated the seventy miles home.

Not only did Sam ferry Peter to doctors' appointments, he also rewired our house in order to put a phone line in Pete's room. Sam hoped being online would make it easier for Peter to keep in contact with his college friends. Sadly, Peter didn't live long enough to use Sam's gift.

Every night for the two weeks Pete was hospitalized in Portland, Sam and Justine chauffeured me back and forth. After work, they would pick me up and we'd embark on the long trip to be with Pete. Dave, often with Andy and Amy, would already be at the hospital when we arrived. My personal drivers eliminated the need to battle city traffic, lowering my stress level. But more importantly, their support buoyed my battered spirit. And Sam and Justine's effort to get the family all together uplifted Peter, as well.

In Pete's last week of life, this time in Seaside Hospital, Sam and Justine continued their efforts to ease our burdens. Taking care of the practical needs we faced, they brought sandwiches and snacks so we wouldn't have to leave Pete's bedside. If something needed to be done, they were willing and ready to do it.

In Pete's last hours of life, roles were reversed. The youngest went first, leading the way, taking his love for his brother with him and leaving a legacy pointing to Christ. Before he left, Pete gently spoke with Sam of the great times they had shared. They planned a barn-raising in heaven to celebrate when Sam joins him again.

Referring to the way Pete died, Sam plainly insists, "I know what I saw." And what Sam saw changed his life, turning his heart toward heaven.

⌒

Perfect submission, perfect delight,
Visions of rapture now burst on my sight;
Angels descending bring from above
Echoes of mercy, whispers of love.

—Fanny J. Crosby,
"Blessed Assurance"

Hi Peter,

I just talked to your mom an hour or so ago. She indicated you were feeling better since coming home from the hospital. That's great to hear. It must be difficult to face another treatment so soon, knowing the agony that comes with it. Each day seems to bring you another challenge to meet: physically, mentally, and spiritually.

The Bible is filled with stories of God testing the character, faith, obedience, love, and loyalty of his people. Words like trials, temptations, testing, and refining occur more than two hundred times in the Bible. Adam and Eve were tempted when they had to decide whether or not to eat the forbidden fruit. Repeatedly, Abraham and Sarah were tried, especially when Abraham was asked to sacrifice their son, Isaac. Joseph and David were often put through trials. The early Christians endured the Roman persecution.

But perhaps the greatest test is when God seems to have abandoned us. King Hezekiah faced this particular trial: "God withdrew from Hezekiah in order to test him and to see what was really in his heart" (2 Chron. 32:31 NLT).

Pete, your cancer is a test that develops and reveals your character. Every shot, every ache, and every indignity you must endure refines and displays your character. All of it has eternal significance, preparing you for what's to come.

Every time you pass a test, God makes plans to reward you in heaven. James says that "God blesses the people who patiently endure testing. Afterward they will receive the crown of life that God has promised to those who love him" (James 1:12 NLT).

Pete, you have already passed numerous tests. You've done it in the classroom, the athletic arena, in personal relationships, and in your previous bout with cancer. Because you passed these tests, Christ is more visible in you. Your current trial, a matter of life and death, is overwhelmingly hard, but with God's help you will pass it, too. "No test or temptation that comes your way is beyond the course of what others have had to face. All you need to remember is that God will never let you down; he'll never let you be pushed past your limit; he'll always be there to help you come through it" (1 Cor. 10:13 MSG).

God is helping you, Pete. This test will end; your reward is waiting. For us "to live is Christ and to die is gain" (Phil. 1:21).

I love you,
Uncle Don

Remember every road that GOD led you on for those forty years in the wilderness, pushing you to your limits, testing you so that he would know what you were made of, whether you would keep his commandments or not. He put you through hard times. He made you go hungry. Then he fed you with manna, something neither you nor your parents knew anything about, so you would learn that men and women don't live by bread only; we live by every word that comes from GOD's mouth. (Deut. 8:2–3 MSG)

9

Fear

WHILE Peter was in grade school, anxiety and panic attacks crippled me—my stomach churned and my heart pounded with dread if Dave or the boys were out of my sight. Even with them safe and sound at home, I never totally relaxed. Fear of death stripped me of happiness and contentment. I constantly fought to protect my family from danger—and in my mind almost everything was a danger. Just putting the boys on the school bus seemed an extreme risk. An accident lay in wait on every curve of our twisting country road.

This excessive paranoia contributed to depression. I knew I should be enjoying life—yet constant apprehension made me miserable. I believed in God, but failed to trust him with the lives of loved ones. Unconsciously, I feared God's plan for them might not coincide with mine—and that was not okay.

Peter entered middle school without encountering any major catastrophes, allowing my phobias to gradually lessen. Shortly before he was diagnosed with ocular melanoma in high school, my fears had dropped to a fairly comfortable level. Not where they should be, perhaps, but much improved.

The removal of Pete's eye brought death to the forefront once again. Yet surprisingly, the staggering fear didn't reappear, despite the fifty-fifty odds of him surviving his teens or early twenties. Knowing I couldn't control or even influence whether the cancer metastasized, I gave up fooling myself. It wasn't as simple as keeping him off the school bus any longer. Instead of striving to shield him, I concentrated on ensuring that Pete lived as normally as possible, supporting his participation in sports and other activities, even letting him drive with one eye. I was finally figuring out God has to do the protecting.

When cancer showed up in Pete's liver, my pain was intense, but, strangely, fear wasn't an overriding emotion. I prayed for God to guard Pete's faith. His life was ending—nothing mattered more than his relationship with Christ. Above all, I wanted him ready for eternity. God was the only viable option; I had to trust him with Pete.

And God did protect Pete. I wouldn't bring him back even if it were in my means to do so. He's safe forever—exactly what I had hoped for him. The security I'd longed for was right and good. I just hadn't grasped that it could only be fully achieved in heaven.

Experiencing God's power and love as Pete died completed my change of heart. I've found freedom in trusting God with my family, enabling me to relax and embrace life more than ever. I accept the accompanying hazards and joys this world brings—thoroughly convinced heaven is waiting at the end of the road for both my loved ones and me.

⌐

> Out of the fear and dread of the tomb,
> Jesus, I come, Jesus, I come;
> Into the joy and light of Thy home,
> Jesus, I come to Thee.
> Out of depths of ruin untold,
> Into the peace of Thy sheltering fold,
> Ever Thy glorious face to behold,
> Jesus, I come to Thee.
>
> —William T. Sleeper,
> "Out of My Bondage, Sorrow and Night"

May 11, 1998

Dear Peter,

My day off has been busy. Ellie and I spent much of the day doing yard work. I hauled several loads of dirt to make mounds and raised flowerbeds. Afterward I mowed the lawn and began laying a flagstone walkway. Ellie is continually planting more flowers and bushes. The foxglove from Hamlet is thriving. Ellie's gift for gardening makes our home more beautiful.

God has showered you with gifts, Pete, including your exceptional mind, quiet leadership, and athletic ability. They are given by God to be used for his purposes. Peter, how you manage what God has given to you here in the land of the dying will pay dividends in the land of the living.

Do you remember the parable of the talents, the man who leaves on a trip, entrusting his resources to three employees? Upon his return, he asks the men to account for the money left with them. The two who invested wisely are praised and rewarded: "Well done, my good and faithful servant. You have been faithful in handling this small amount, so now I will give you many more responsibilities. Let's celebrate together!" (Matt. 25:21 NLT).

God promises three rewards to faithful managers when they arrive in heaven. First, you will receive God's commendation: He'll say, "Way to go, Pete! Well done!" Next, God will promote you and give you greater responsibilities for all eternity: "I will put you in charge of many things." Finally, he will make you the guest of honor at a special party: "Let's rejoice together!"[1]

I think about this almost every day. I long to hear God say, "Good job, Don!" I reflect on it when I face a decision on how to use my time. It runs through my mind when I have opportunities to help others. It gives meaning and direction to every aspect of my life. More than anything, I want to make wise investments of my life and resources so there is a return when I'm called home.

Our lives take on greater meaning when we realize how closely they're linked to eternity. Whatever time God gives you, Pete, invest it in his eternal kingdom. Live every day for Jesus, so you'll have no regrets, whether you live a short time or to a ripe old age. Then like Paul, you can honestly say, "To live is Christ and to die is gain" (Phil. 1:21).

Peter, this expresses the deepest conviction of my heart. I hope your heart resonates with it. I don't know of anything more important to give you. I share these truths as an expression of my love and care for you.

Also living for Christ,
Uncle Don

Don't store up treasures here on earth, where they can be eaten by moths and get rusty, and where thieves break in and steal. Store your treasures in heaven, where they will never become moth-eaten or rusty and where they will be safe from thieves. Wherever your treasure is, there your heart and thoughts will also be. (Matt. 6:19–21 NLT)

10

Infinite Joy

PETE knew the exhilarating joy of victory. Whether scoring the winning touchdown in football or breaking a track record in the 400-meter dash, he competed hard for the win. I love watching a videotape of Pete; his arms triumphantly pump the air as he leaps and bounds down the basketball court, celebrating a last minute win with his teammates, elation bursting over his face and in every movement of his body. There's nothing quite like the taste of victory.

Seaside High's win at the state championship football game at the University of Oregon's football stadium in Eugene vaulted the players into hometown-hero status. As the game clock expired, Seaside fans mobbed the field while the announcer yelled, again and again, "Off the field, spectators stay off the field!" But the tide of jubilant Seasiders wouldn't be denied the pleasure of joining their team in the celebration. From the grandstand, tingling with pride, I watched Pete, hands above his head, being crushed and embraced by the impassioned crowd. Exuberance filled the whole team.

Later that icy, starry night, half of the town met the returning team's bus a few miles outside of Seaside. Cars lined both sides of the highway for as far as we could see. Waving, ecstatic boys hung out the bus windows as the driver slowed to a crawl through the tunnel of flashing lights and honking horns. Sirens screaming, fire trucks and police cars led the returning heroes and their fans to the high school. The sweet aroma of victory delivered just the tiniest hint of heaven.

But the magic of that night dimmed to an occasional memory. Life went on, leaving fleeting glories in the dust. No longer in the winner's circle, Pete's teammates and friends struggle with the cares of this world. Not so for Pete.

Peter is immersed in boundless joy that only increases as he dives deeper into the wonders of heaven. The thrill of winning the state championship game faded, but Pete's final victory shines brighter with each day spent in paradise. Hope of such endless delight pulls me on toward the finish line.

Joy is the serious business of heaven.[1]

⌒

> There are depths of love that I cannot know
> 'Til I cross the narrow sea;
> There are heights of joy that I may not reach
> 'Til I rest in peace with Thee.
>
> —Fanny J. Crosby,
> "I Am Thine, O Lord"

Hi Nephew,

My mind has been wandering back to your high school football days. One of my regrets is being unable to attend your state championship game. Living in Arizona at the time, I missed all the excitement. But I was thrilled to watch a game the following year. After meeting your folks for dinner in Scappoose, we made our way to the stadium to watch you play.

At one point, Seaside had the ball on its own four-yard line. I think it was second down. I leaned over and said to your mom and dad, "Watch this! Pete will get the ball and take it all the way." Then you guys left the huddle to line up. After the snap, the quarterback handed you the ball. Breaking several tackles, you sprinted ninety-six yards to score a touchdown, setting a school record for the longest run from line of scrimmage. Wow!

What a contrast between now and those days of winning championships and scoring touchdowns. It seemed as if you could do almost anything you tried. You were strong and fast. Now taking a few steps zaps all your energy. But even if you didn't have cancer, your days of competing in football would end. Like one's days of playing football, life is temporary. You must be keenly aware of how quickly life is passing by.

Job said, "Our days on earth are as transient as a

shadow" (Job 8:9 NLT). And David prayed, "LORD, remind me how brief my time on earth will be. Remind me that my days are numbered, and that my life is fleeing away" (Ps. 39:4 NLT). It's significant that David asked God to constantly remind him that life on earth rushes rapidly by. Over the centuries, believers intentionally cultivated this mentality. Stonecutters etched the words "Consider your own death" on walls in many of the great cathedrals in Europe.

In our age, most people seek to ignore evidence that life is fleeting. But if people live with an awareness that this present life passes very quickly, they are able to maintain a perspective on what really matters. Scoring touchdowns is wonderful, but it doesn't seem very significant in the long run.

The Declaration of Independence proclaims that God has given every person unalienable rights, including "life, liberty, and the pursuit of happiness." I value these privileges but believe God doesn't intend for us to find complete happiness in this present life. While living in the land of the dying, no one is totally content. Here we experience all kinds of hardships and suffering. Occasionally we get a little taste of what could be—winning a championship, scoring touchdowns, falling in love, accomplishing a goal, enjoying family and friendships. They whet our appetites for the joys to come. While we only taste a morsel here, we'll feast on them daily in heaven.

If we fully experienced the wonders of heaven here, we would want this world to remain our home. But God desires us to live in anticipation of our real home. So we turn our hearts toward heaven instead of focusing all our desires on the things of this life. When we die, we won't leave home, but go home. "For to me, to live is Christ and to die is gain" (Phil. 1:21).

Love,
Uncle Don

I have told you all this so that you may have peace in me. Here on earth you will have many trials and sorrows. But take heart, because I have overcome the world. (John 16:33 NLT)

11

When Dreams Come True

DURING Pete's illness, I conjured vivid images of special events made complete by Pete's presence. To be picture-perfect, Andy and Kari's August wedding needed all three brothers standing together. How could the ceremony occur without him? And one more Christmas, just one more with Pete. These visions repeatedly played in my mind's eye and heart.

Of my boys, Peter most enjoyed the glittery trimmings and traditions of Christmas. Andy and I called Peter at college the December before he came home for his last Christmas. Teasing Pete, Andy said, "This year we aren't going to have a tree and all the other unnecessary tinsel associated with Christmas. We'll celebrate the real meaning of Christ's birth." The following week Peter called. "Mom, when I come home there *will* be a tree, won't there?" Of course there was.

In March, I learned we'd probably spent our last Christmas with Pete. Still, I clung to the dream of another holiday together, a lovely, fairy-tale story, every detail sparkling and alive with wonder and love. Hope as I might, this imaginary Christmas failed to shield me from the horrid reality at hand.

Late in May, as sickness took its toll on Peter's body, Andy and

Pete discussed ways for Pete to still participate in the wedding. If Pete could generate enough energy to walk to the front of the church, a chair would be waiting for him, allowing him to sit through the ceremony. Another possibility was using a wheelchair.

But Pete's health slipped away daily, leaving him couch-bound. Gathering the oomph to drag himself to the bathroom or to bed was the best he could manage. Imagining him journeying to Portland for the rehearsal and groom's dinner, then enduring the exhausting wedding day seemed far-fetched. Still, picturing the day without Peter was unbearable.

So I dreamed on of Peter mustering the strength to sit in a wheelchair for the wedding. By renting a motel room near the reception building, I thought, Pete might catch a nap and be refreshed enough to get through the festivities. I envisioned splitting time between him in the motel and Andy and Kari's reception. Not the best solution, but one that included Peter.

My dreams didn't materialize. Peter died seven weeks before the wedding and six months before Christmas. The wedding was beautiful, yet for me terribly sad. Saying Peter was irreplaceable, Andy left an empty spot next to him during the ceremony, the spot where Peter would have stood between his brothers. Our family lit a candle in Peter's memory, including him in the ceremony the only way we could. When Christmas rolled around, I unpacked the lights and decorations thinking, "Yes, Peter, there will be a tree for you, even if I'm not feeling the holiday spirit." That's the way it is now: Pete is absent, the dreams unfulfilled.

But somehow, Peter's death has left me a grander, fuller, more perfect hope than I thought possible. In many ways, it's a wonderful relief to understand that I wasn't made for this world, and neither was Peter. God had a spot in heaven, as Andy did in his wedding, which only Pete could fill. Peter is living in a world that never disappoints. I yearn for the time I join him there. So, until that day, I'll seek to live for Christ, knowing unimaginable delights wait in a place where our heartfelt dreams become real.

What rejoicing in His presence,
When are banished grief and pain;
When the crooked ways are straightened,
And the dark things shall be plain.

Face to face I shall behold Him,
Far beyond the starry sky;
Face to face in all His glory,
I shall see Him by and by!

—Carrie E. Breck,
"Face to Face with Christ, My Savior"

May 15, 1998

Dear Pete,

I assume that you are feeling pretty punk today after all the shots you've had to give yourself. Those treatments must make the old two-a-day football practices seem like a walk in the park. The thought of injecting myself in the stomach makes my knees weak. Your courage and strength continue to inspire me. Yet I know it is God's power being manifested in your weakness, helping and strengthening you to face these challenges daily.

It's almost as though I can actually see God working in your life, which may sound strange since I haven't been to Hamlet for several weeks. When I pray and think about you, a clear picture forms in my mind. You're lying on the couch in the family room, with Amy by your side. Your folks are coming in and out to chat, as well as to check on you. I can almost hear the brotherly teasing during Sam's and Andy's frequent visits. But regardless of who is with you, Jesus fills the room. I can't visualize him physically but can sense his presence.

Pete, do you feel the Lord there with you? Is his spirit so tangible, sometimes you think you can reach out and touch him? He is with you. But his spiritual presence is detected only by faith. I have walked into many rooms, in both hospitals and homes, and known immediately that Jesus was there. I can't explain it, but I know it.

A young woman in the hospital, near death, wanted to celebrate the Lord's Supper with her family and friends. I went to find a roll and juice in the cafeteria. When I returned, I immediately sensed something had changed. There was a Holy Presence. I asked the woman if Jesus had come. "Yes, he came and stood there," she replied, pointing to the foot of her bed. She obviously had seen something that no one else had. God's peace pervaded the room in a new, unmistakable way.

The Old Testament tells of the King of Aram's troops surrounding the city of Dothan at night with the intention of capturing the prophet Elisha. The following morning, Elisha's servant was shocked to discover the enemy army encircling them. He raced to Elisha in a panic:

> "Don't be afraid!" Elisha told him. "For there are more on our side than on theirs!" Then Elisha prayed, "O LORD, open his eyes and let him see!" The LORD opened his servant's eyes, and when he looked up, he saw that the hillside around Elisha was filled with horses and chariots of fire. (2 Kings 6:16-17 NLT)

The story concludes with the enemy surrendering and being sent home unharmed. God was there, whether or not he was visible.

He is there with you, too. As Elisha prayed for his servant, I pray for you, "Lord, open Peter's eyes and let him see." So look to Jesus, and look for Jesus. You may be surprised at what happens. When your eyes are opened to spiritual reality, you too can say, "For to me, to live is Christ and to die is gain" (Phil. 1:21).

God loves you and so do I,
Uncle Don

Keep your eyes on Jesus, who both began and finished this race we're in. Study how he did it. Because he never lost sight of where he was headed—that exhilarating finish in and with God—he could put up with anything along the way: cross, shame, whatever. And now he's *there*, in the place of honor, right alongside God. (Heb. 12:2 MSG)

12

Needles

NEEDLES were a hated part of Peter's illness. Yet biopsies, blood work, shots, and IVs became an inescapable routine in his life. It was a needle biopsy that positively identified Peter's liver cancer.

Dave and I were allowed the dubious honor of witnessing the biopsy procedure. Uncharacteristically, Pete asked about the possibility of an anesthetic, and much to his distress he was told none was necessary. The biopsy didn't go well; Peter's well-toned body worked against him, and the doctor had difficulty pushing the needle through his strong abdominal muscles. Watching Pete lying on the table, his pale face dripping sweat, seeing five to eight inches of bloody needle drawn from his stomach time after time made me woozy. Finishing the procedure was a short-lived relief. At the next doctor's appointment, he was informed that the biopsy had been a failure and needed to be repeated in order to extract viable tissue. Pete was not happy, but a dose of Valium made the second biopsy easier to endure.

Hoping to bolster his immune system and prolong his life, Peter reluctantly learned to give himself shots of interferon and interleukin-2. Sitting at the kitchen table, he'd swab his stomach with rubbing alcohol, unwillingly pick up the syringe and stare at it distastefully, then lay it back on the table. Sometimes he'd place it on his stomach before putting it down again. Finally, slowly spinning the needle between his thumb and fingers, he'd gradually work it under his skin. At last, courage built up, he'd push the plunger.

His aversion to administering his own shots grew as he came to know the horrid side effects that awaited him. An hour after injecting himself, Pete was on the couch, buried deeply in blankets, gripped with violent flu-like symptoms. Shaking uncontrollably, teeth chattering, he couldn't get warm until the effects of the medication wore off.

Within weeks, once again connected to IVs, Peter lay dying in Seaside Hospital. Needles and tubes no longer bothered him; he'd grown so accustomed to them. At one point during his last night, a nurse offered Pete pain medication. With a little smile, Pete responded, "No need." Returning his smile, she tossed the medicine in the trash can. His earthly trials were almost over, and he was looking forward. When God said, "Pete, it's time," Pete sat up in bed, powerfully swept his arms back and forth and, with tremendous joy, flew home. His strong arms sent the IVs, an unnecessary link to illness and pain, crashing to the floor. In heaven, cancer, needles, and hospitals don't exist. Pete is gloriously free from all that hurts.

⌒

Jesus, lover of my soul, let me to Thy bosom fly,
While the nearer waters roll, while the tempest still is high.
Hide me, O my Savior, hide, till the storm of life is past;
Safe into the haven guide; O receive my soul at last.

—Charles Wesley,
"Jesus, Lover of My Soul"

May 18, 1998

Hi Pete,

I've been working in the yard again today. For me, digging in the garden, playing a round of golf, and just running errands are nice breaks from my regular work schedule. I wish you could get a day's respite from your illness, but cancer is with you 24/7.

Discussing day-to-day events seems frivolous in comparison to what you're enduring. But then, sometimes I worry my letters are too intense. I have chosen to err on the side of being too serious rather than superficial. I don't want death to become the proverbial elephant in the living room that no one mentions, so I'll continue to talk about it.

Peter, I'd like to share some more thoughts about spiritual vision, living with an eternal perspective. Spiritually blind people see only what's right in front of them: the material world, without an awareness of the spiritual realm. They miss much of what is happening, because it can't be perceived through the five senses. In contrast, believers see beyond the present physical realm to the eternal. "All these faithful ones died without receiving what God had promised them, but they saw it all from a distance and welcomed the promises of God" (Heb. 11:13 NLT).

Without an eternal outlook, spiritually blind people can only live in denial (refusing to face the possibility of death), wallow in self-pity, or just stoically bear suffering. But Pete, since you see your present circumstances from the viewpoint of eternity, you experience hope, joy, and peace. You can find certainty in the face of uncertainty, knowing cancer is not the last word. Through faith you see beyond suffering to heaven.

Paul says it this way: "We don't look at the troubles we can see right now; rather, we look forward to what we have not yet seen. For the troubles we see will soon be over, but the joys to come will last forever" (2 Cor. 4:18 NLT).

Look forward, beyond your illness, recognizing that "our present troubles are quite small and won't last very long. Yet they produce for us an immeasurably great glory that will last forever!" (2 Cor. 4:17 NLT). This is not a pie-in-the-sky wish, but God's written promise to you.

Pete, look at life and death through the lens of faith. Live in anticipation of the joys to come that will last forever. Then if God takes away your cancer and gives you many more years on earth, you will live them with purpose and joy. But if God removes you from this land of the dying, you will be prepared. "For to me, to live is Christ and to die is gain" (Phil. 1:21).

Looking forward in faith,
Uncle Don

———

Let heaven fill your thoughts. Do not think only about things down here on earth. For you died when Christ died, and your real life is hidden with Christ in God. And when Christ, who is your real life, is revealed to the whole world, you will share in all his glory. (Col. 3:2–4 NLT)

Peter's first birthday, June 5, 1978.

Sam, Peter, and Andy on Sugar; Dave holding the reins, Christmas 1981.

Family portrait in 1982 (*from left to right*): Andy, Charlotte, Sam, Peter, and Dave.

Family gathering at Hamlet in 1986: Peter (*left*) and his cousin Sean in the foreground, Uncle Don in the background to the left.

Peter, eighth grade football.

Peter, Christmas 1994.

Peter running the final leg in the state championship 4 x 400 relay in his junior year.

Peter and Amy dolled up for the junior/senior prom, Peter's junior year, 1995.

Peter, senior basketball.

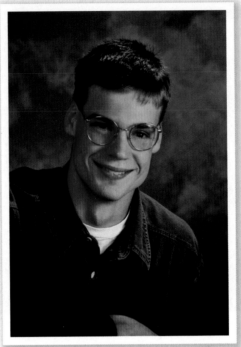

Peter's high school graduation photo, 1996.

Peter enjoying his last fishing trip a month before he died, so weak he was barely able to get from the boat back to the truck.

From left to right: Amy, Dave, Charlotte, Sam, and Andy lighting a candle in Peter's memory at Andy's wedding, seven weeks after Peter's death.

From left to right: Peter's grandma, Charlotte, Dave, Sam, Justine, Andy, and Kari in the missing man formation, 1999.

Peter's brothers and sisters-in-law in 2001 (*from left to right*): Sam and Justine, Andy and Kari.

Charlotte and Dave putting Christmas greens on Peter's grave, 2001.

13

Missing You

TERRA, Amy's fifteen-year-old sister, loved Peter as if he were her brother. While still in high school, she wrote an essay about him:

Peter James

When he came to our house after work, he always smelled like Christmas trees. Towering over me, he stood with faded Levis, simple T-shirts, and a short, clean, to-the-point haircut. He read a lot of Ernest Hemingway. He picked at his food before deciding the best way to eat it. He had a low voice but spoke with strength, and I clung to every word, every syllable. Admiring him, I was Amy's younger sister—Little Terra. That was me. I talked to him about track or basketball and my high school dilemmas that he freshly remembered. I made him laugh.

He was stretched out on our gray couch when I last saw him. I sat next to him and blackened in the teeth of the movie stars on the cover of the new *TV Guide*. He laughed at my little makeovers. . . . I don't have any memories more recent than him sitting on that couch, picking the feathers out of a big blue pillow and watching me deface Oprah on the cover of the *TV Guide*.

I was afraid to see him after that. I didn't go to the

hospital. He never made his bed, and I didn't want to see him restricted by those rigid, unyielding hospital corners. I'm sure he didn't complain, though. He wasn't like that. Somehow Amy could be there, amidst the flowers and cards, and I know he asked her to kiss him again. I'm not sure, but I bet she smiled for him too.

I woke up late the morning after he died. My hair was salty and smelled of smoke from last night's bonfire. I felt kind of sticky under my twisted, blue starry comforter; the day was already so warm.

My dad hugged me, leaving me alone to scream quietly in my room for a while after telling me Peter was gone. I'd never seen him cry before.

Amy hadn't slept. She was sitting straight up in our parents' empty bed, so small, right in the middle, a little girl between two invisible parents after a nightmare. She was so fragile, but she hugged me real tight when I cried in the doorway. She combed my hair with her fingers as I cried on her shoulder. I made her shirt all wet, but then my face was dry for a minute.

Later that morning I drove to a little store by the beach that never got much business. I bought Amy a Sprite. I brought it back home to her with a straw. She took a sip and was through. She thanked me.

I watched part of my sister die that day. I sat by her all day until I was out of tears and when I was, we laughed, and talked, and I braided her long blond hair.

"Amy?" I asked out of the sunlit freckled room, "Does he know that I miss him yet?"

She spoke easily without opening her eyes. "Yep."

She was holding onto a picture. I curled up next to her like a cat and smelled the sunlight on my tears.[1]

Yep, Peter knows we miss him. He knew it as he died. He knew, and spoke of the reunion to come. He knew, and asked us to find comfort in Christ. Hope lives. Love endures.

⌒

Does Jesus care when I've said "good-bye"
To the dearest on earth to me,
And my sad heart aches till it nearly breaks,
Is it aught to Him? Does He see?

O yes, He cares, I know He cares,
His heart is touched with my grief;
When the days are weary, the long nights dreary,
I know my Savior cares.
—Frank E. Graeff,
"Does Jesus Care?"

Hi Peter,

I hope you're feeling a little better after completing your last treatment. Sometimes I find myself wondering how I'd react to such suffering. Would I lose heart?

This brings to mind a young man named Matt in my congregation.[2] He shared many stories with me about his hate-filled brother, Josh, a self-described Marxist who despised Christians. Josh had once tried to set fire to the family home while his parents and brothers slept. Hiring a security company to guard the house became necessary. One day Matt asked me to accompany him on a visit to his alienated brother.

With some fear, I agreed to go. What a wild time! Enraged when I mentioned Christ, Josh shouted and swore at me. He slugged me in the face, giving me a fat lip and bloody nose, all the while screaming he would kill me. Matt tackled his brother from behind, shouting for me to run. I did! As I fled, Josh continued threatening to kill me if I didn't renounce Christ. Moments later, Matt caught up with me, and we sped away.

Through years of Josh's hatred and threats, Matt persistently reached out to his brother. He was the only family member maintaining contact with Josh, desiring to share Christ with him. Despite demoralizing circumstances, Matt didn't lose heart.

In the Bible, losing heart means becoming discouraged to the point of giving up. Fear, suffering, and seemingly insurmountable problems often bring such feelings. In ministry, I struggle with discouragement, having started down the road to losing heart on several occasions. When people become so overwhelmed that they lose faith, it is the spiritual equivalent of cancer. Problems seem bigger than God. Perspective is lost. At the end of the road, faith is lost. The apostle Peter must have lost heart on the night he denied Jesus three times, but he "took heart" when the resurrected Christ showed himself to him.

I have a favorite Scripture verse I go to when my heart feels like it's shriveling up within me. When joy disappears. When fear replaces faith. It's as if a python wraps itself around my chest, squeezing the life out of me. Then I read, "We do not lose heart. Though outwardly we are wasting away, yet inwardly we are being renewed day by day" (2 Cor. 4:16).

I hope you do not struggle with losing heart. Here's a great promise for any Christian who is suffering, perhaps to the point of death: "Our light and momentary troubles are achieving for us an eternal glory that far outweighs them all" (2 Cor. 4:17). If you read the entire passage of 2 Corinthians 4:7-18, you'll see that the light and momentary troubles Paul faced were not light at all. They seemed that way only because Paul saw the big picture. He had an eternal perspective. For him, living meant Christ and dying was gain.

I pray you will never lose heart, but instead take heart. I ask God to keep your faith strong, even as your body grows weaker.

Your uncle, but also your brother in Christ,
Don

Therefore we do not lose heart. Though outwardly we are wasting away, yet inwardly we are being renewed day by day. For our light and momentary troubles are achieving for us an eternal glory that far outweighs them all. So we fix our eyes not on what is seen, but on what is unseen. For what is seen is temporary, but what is unseen is eternal. (2 Cor. 4:16–18)

14

Losses

LITTLE by little, the years following Peter's death meant losing concrete ties to him. I didn't know the losses would continue to mount in countless small ways. I mourned each as the days stretched to years.

The summer he died, I would go into his room—surrounding myself with the clothes he wore, the objects he touched, the music he listened to, and the books he read. I'd close my eyes and breathe in his lingering scent—a blend of deodorant, soap, and shampoo that was uniquely Pete. Then one morning, I entered his room and was dismayed to discover the smell had vanished as if he hadn't lived there for the last twenty-one years. The tears fell as I said good-bye to another tangible part of him.

Ordinary chores struck me with intense grief that took me by surprise. Vacuuming, dusting, and changing the sheets on his bed in preparation for company sent me into a tailspin. This was Pete's room, yet I readied it for guests—not for him. How sad to recognize my days of cleaning for his return were over—Pete wouldn't be coming home again.

And I never dreamed scrubbing walls could be traumatic until I began the task of washing the staircase. As I stood on scaffolding that Dave had erected, sponge and cleanser in hand, it suddenly dawned on me I was erasing Pete's handprints. The image of him jumping as high as he could and slapping the wall as he bounded down the steps filled me with longing to see him. Yet, swipe by swipe, I eradicated proof he had lived, loved, and matured within these walls. One more connection to Pete severed.

Packing and disposing of his clothes and personal belongings cut to the quick. Part of me knew it was necessary, while another part clung to anything Peter. Item by item, I relegated his possessions to his brothers, friends, Goodwill, or the garbage heap. One tattered, old, gray T-shirt that Justine had given him on his fourteenth birthday found its way to the ragbag. He had worn that shirt for years. I retrieved it later, tucking it neatly away in a drawer—ensuring Peter's favorite shirt wouldn't be used and discarded as unimportant.

I frequently visited Pete's grave. For two or three years, I'd often find tokens left by his friends—flowers, notes, a pile of carefully stacked stones, seashells, a lock of his girlfriend's blond hair. One visit I found a framed picture of him with his middle school basketball team—the attached card read, "I miss you, Buddy." The offerings dried up as time quietly slipped by, breaking my heart a bit more, withering another tie to Pete.

Family photographs fill our home, the ones of Peter unchanging; he doesn't grow older like Sam and Andy. I treasure my memories—yet they're part of the past, beyond restoring—I need more. I want a future with a living, breathing, vibrant, dynamic Pete. A Pete I can touch, talk, and laugh with—and, yes, even smell. Praise God, that day will come.

⌣

Soft as the voice of an angel,
Breathing a lesson unheard,
Hope with a gentle persuasion
Whispers her comforting word:
Wait till the darkness is over,
Wait till the tempest is done,

Losses

Hope for the sunshine tomorrow,
After the shower is gone.

Whispering hope, oh how welcome thy voice,
Making my heart in its sorrow rejoice.
—Alice Hawthorne [Septimus Winner],
"Whispering Hope"

Good morning Peter,

I woke up thinking about you, wishing we could share a leisurely breakfast on our patio. It would be wonderful to sit with you, sipping a cup of coffee, talking and taking in Mount Rainier's early morning majesty. It's so easy to take such everyday pleasures for granted. Your illness reminds me to savor the small, ordinary things in life.

Too often I fail to appreciate God's grace. Like the air around me, I rarely think about it—until I visit my friend with emphysema. Seeing her gasping for air makes me grateful for every breath. Similarly, God's grace constantly surrounds and fills me even though I'm usually oblivious to it.

Grace is simple to define, but elusive to grasp. It means unmerited favor, getting something good I don't deserve. That goodness includes God's love, forgiveness, and acceptance. Christ is the ultimate gift of grace. Always freely given, like air, grace can't be earned, bought, or borrowed. Merely believe and so receive it.

Simple, huh? Like I said, grace is easy to define but challenging to hold on to, particularly for terminally ill people. Guilt feelings make heaven seem like a mirage, something that teases them, always just beyond their reach. God's grace is the antidote for guilt—obliterating it, and then filling its place with peace and joy.

I know a kind, gentle widower who looks after single moms and the elderly. I love this guy—he genuinely cares about those who are alone. Nearing eighty, he realizes he doesn't have much time left. Yet death scares this dear man. His problem goes back to the Second World War when he was a marine in the South Pacific. In the heat of a fierce battle, he crossed the line and did horrible things he can't forget.

Guilt, shame, and regret have plagued him for over fifty years, causing him to despise himself. He naturally assumes that God feels the same way. Since his actions were inexcusable, he reasons they must also be unforgivable, making God seem distant and unapproachable.

Trapped by his feelings of unworthiness, he's spent years punishing himself for what happened in the past. Yet the Bible teaches God's grace is greater than our sins. My widower friend has to believe this before the chains holding him captive can be broken, freeing him to experience true peace and the certainty that Christ is waiting for him in heaven. Jesus paid the price; this man only has to accept the gift.

Pete, cancer can steal your health and even your life, but don't let it steal your peace and your assurance of heaven. The apostle Paul, before meeting Jesus, was an accessory to murder. He hated Christ and ruthlessly hunted down Christians, seeking to imprison them. But after his conversion, Paul was free to exclaim, "For to me, to live is Christ and to die is gain" (Phil. 1:21). No guilt, only peace and confidence.

Hang in there, Pete. Your guilt is also nailed to the cross, so bask in the peace that comes from knowing that Jesus loves and forgives you.

Also secure in his grace,
Uncle Don

—

But because of his great love for us, God, who is rich in mercy, made us alive with Christ even when we were dead in transgressions—it is by grace you have been saved. And God raised us up with Christ and seated us with him in the heavenly realms in Christ Jesus, in order that in the coming ages he might show the incomparable riches of his grace, expressed in his kindness to us in Christ Jesus. For it is by grace you have been saved, through faith—and this not from yourselves, it is the gift of God—not by works, so that no one can boast. (Eph. 2:4–9)

15

Supporting Pete

THOSE of us who loved Peter were united in our desire to help him through his suffering. In retrospect, doing some things differently may have smoothed his journey a bit, although they wouldn't have changed the final outcome.

In a mistaken attempt to shield Pete, we avoided discussing with doctors two key questions. First, what was Pete's life expectancy? Second, how much time could we hope to gain through chemotherapy? These unasked questions led Pete to believe he had much more time than he really did, and possibly affected the medical decisions we made. Only after the completion of chemo did we learn Peter's expected life span was three to six months from the time of diagnosis; and in the unlikely event chemo slowed his cancer at all, the doctors would have considered it successful with weeks added to his life.

Looking back, undergoing chemo doesn't seem wrong. For someone who was only twenty, even the tiniest chance seemed worth a try. Conversely, given the dismal odds, it wouldn't have been wrong if we'd chosen to forego treatment, perhaps lessening some of Peter's suffering. More information could have helped us as we made tough choices.

Knowing there were times when Pete wanted to candidly talk about the most likely scenario, I wish I'd sought more opportunities to discuss his condition and the reality of life with Christ after death. Dwelling on death wouldn't have benefited him, but the few occasions we openly spoke of dying helped Pete endure suffering with hope. Dave often prayed and read Scripture with Pete, but he avoided the topic of dying. While Dave's steadfast faith upheld Peter, he now regrets missed chances to strengthen Pete's belief in the wonders awaiting him in paradise.

Peter received a card filled with messages praising God for Pete's restored health. It came from a church group who had prayed, believing that God would heal Peter because of their faith. Peter's reaction bordered on irritation. "I still have cancer," he said. "Sure, miracles happen, but where have they left room for God's will and purpose for my life? Do they know more than he does about what's best for me?" The many other cards Pete received lifted his spirits, but this well-intended note backfired.

Several good-hearted people had an artificial optimism when visiting Pete, whitewashing the situation with forced laughter and a sunny, "everything's dandy" attitude. Their inability to face the fact that nothing was fine, good, or fun in his life separated them from Pete. He didn't need gloomy friends or family around him, just honest people who were sensitive to his plight. He enjoyed laughing and talking about things that took his mind off cancer, but not while blindly pretending the present circumstances were rosy.

The best we could do was be there, gently loving Pete and pointing him to God. Our efforts to help him were not always perfect, but the promise "My grace is sufficient for you, for my power is made perfect in weakness" (2 Cor. 12:9) proved to be true. God didn't let Pete down but gave him wings to fly.

Supporting Pete

⌒

Through many dangers, toils and snares,
I have already come;
'Tis grace that brought me safe thus far,
And grace will lead me home.
> —John Newton,
> "Amazing Grace"

May 23, 1998

Dear Peter,

You're never far from my thoughts and constantly in my prayers as you battle cancer. What a privilege to have you as my nephew. Measured by miles, we're far apart, but I feel close because of our bond in Christ. God's love and power give me confidence to ask him for your healing. In all my petitions, there is a sense of expectancy, yet my prayers are bathed in tears of pain because I care so much.

So many people are praying for you, Peter. Only God knows how many prayer chains around the country are interceding on your behalf. But there's a mystery surrounding it all. Prayer is not a formula forcing God to grant us our requests. Those who take this approach confuse prayer with magic. Magic is the belief that doing a prescribed thing— saying the right words, doing specific actions—guarantees the results we want.

Prayer is a conversation, not the placing of an order. It is coming close to God, opening our hearts to him, and allowing God to speak to us. Yet, even in our boldness, we don't dictate to God. Ultimately, prayer is the means of aligning our will with God's, surrendering our desires to him. Jesus did this in the Garden of Gethsemane when he prayed, "If it is possible, let this cup of suffering be taken away from me. Yet I want your will, not mine" (Matt. 26:39 NLT).

Pete, you obviously understand the purpose of prayer. Whenever people ask how to pray for you, you always respond, "Pray for God's will to be done." It shows your heart is right and your faith is strong. Well-intentioned Christians will inevitably declare that if you pray in faith, you will be healed. Such comments sometimes lead to confusion and discouragement for the one who is ill. Often the patient feels guilty if he isn't healed, thinking it's because he lacks faith. Baloney!

If that were the case, then Jesus lacked faith in the Garden of Gethsemane. It means the millions of martyrs who died over the centuries while refusing to renounce Jesus died in vain—without faith. In truth, their faith was incredibly strong—and yet they were killed. They lived for Christ and death was gain.

There is a time for everything, including "a time to be born and a time to die" (Eccl. 3:2 NLT). The psalmist wrote, "Every day of my life was recorded in your book. Every moment was laid out before a single day had passed" (Ps. 139:16 NLT). Death is not the worst thing for a believer. Quite the opposite—death is the way we move from the land of the dying to the land of the living. Faith lets God decide when the time is right.

You are in my prayers constantly. Think of those who pray for you as the friends who held four corners of a mat to bring the paralyzed man to Jesus. I'm holding one of those corners for you, Peter, praying for you all the time.

I love you,
Uncle Don

Four men arrived carrying a paralyzed man on a mat. They couldn't get to Jesus through the crowd, so they dug through the clay roof above his head. Then they lowered the sick man on his mat, right down in front of Jesus. (Mark 2:3–4 NLT)

16

Tootle-loo, I'll See You There

DURING the time Peter played high school football, Andy and a cousin, Seth, found themselves engaged in a lively discussion regarding the pro and college gridiron. Seth asked, "Who's your favorite player?" Without missing a beat, Andy answered, "Pete." Seth badgered Andy for some famous name. "Come on, who's really your favorite player?" "Pete," persisted Andy. And so it was. Andy never faltered in being Peter's biggest fan on and off the field.

Before Andy departed for college in late September, he helped coach Seaside High football. During Andy's last week of coaching, the normally reserved Peter surprised and touched Andy by praising him in front of the team. "As a boy I loved watching Andy play," said Pete. "It's been my goal to be as great a running back as my brother. He's been my role model. I wear number 23, your number, Andy, in admiration of you."

Andy returned Pete's tribute at his little brother's memorial service. In the following speech, Andy acknowledged the influence Pete had on his life and the hope that Pete had inspired for the future.

Pete's Gifts to Me

Peter was my younger brother. Growing up in a fantastic family, we enjoyed a happy childhood.

As Pete and I matured, so did our relationship. The older we grew, the closer we became. We stayed up late and talked and talked about nothing in particular. Together we learned to catch bass from Cullaby Lake. I'd call him on the phone just to hear his voice. Really seeking and desiring his company, I would get him to run errands with me and drag him along when I visited my friends. He was my brother.

And being brothers was enough. Sam knows what I mean, or maybe anybody with close siblings. The camaraderie is unique and powerful. Being together in all circumstances is special.

Pete's cancer showed up again in his liver this past March, and my attitude remained unchanged from the three and a half years before, when the original tumor was diagnosed in his eye. We were going to beat this thing despite the odds. Even when chemotherapy failed to stop the cancer's proliferation and decimated his blood counts, I continued to be optimistic. With God on our side, I expected something great to happen. I prayed for that even as he battled the pneumonia that he caught twelve days ago, and that killed his body on Saturday.

God certainly had something great in store, but not what I anticipated. Amazed, I witnessed Peter filled to the fullest measure as God's plan came to fruition. When God said, "Pete, let's go," he flew with joy and strength like I've never seen. At his weakest moment, God filled him to overflowing.

These last few days I've considered this miracle, and I'm

excited because I know God has a plan for me, too; I'm going to see what Pete saw and know the same joy he did. So in a way not much has changed. I'm really looking forward to the day I see my brother again, but not just because we're brothers. Now I realize the real camaraderie must be with Jesus, where true fulfillment lies.

Andy's optimism and excitement have only grown since he spoke these words at his brother's memorial. He's a guy who truly enjoys living and has honed the art of having fun, yet our conversations often center on our longing for the freedom and joy we saw in Pete as he entered heaven. "If this life is so good," says Andy, "how can I help but want a world so much bigger and better than I can even imagine? When I see Christ, I'll be made right; I'll belong." With a laugh, he concludes our visits by saying, "Tootle-loo, Mom, I'll see you there!"

⁓

> Finish, then, Thy new creation;
> Pure and spotless let us be.
> Let us see Thy great salvation,
> Perfectly restored in Thee;
> Changed from glory into glory,
> Till in heav'n we take our place,
> Till we cast our crowns before Thee,
> Lost in wonder, love, and praise.
> —Charles Wesley,
> "Love Divine, All Loves Excelling"

May 26, 1998

Hello Pete,

Ellie sends her greetings. It's our nineteenth anniversary, and we spent some time looking at wedding photographs. You were just a little guy with someone holding you in every picture. Sam and Andy were cute little boys, mischief sparkling in their eyes.

Returning from dinner a few minutes ago, a message from your mom on the answering machine let us know you're back in the hospital for a transfusion of platelets. Some setback inevitably seems to follow each good day. Yours is an emotional and spiritual struggle as well as a physical battle. I wish I could do more to help, Peter. Just know that I continue holding my corner of your mat.

Prayers are my way of bringing you to the feet of Jesus, the place where the paralytic was miraculously healed. Over the years I have witnessed a few miracles. They were a regular part, though, of Jesus' ministry, which still continues on earth through those who believe in him.

Yet miracles aren't God's answer for everything. Each person Jesus healed, after the initial spiritual high, had to resume the daily struggles of life in this land of the dying. Every healing in the Bible was, in a sense, temporary because each person who was healed eventually died. There is no lasting remedy until we reach the land of the living. Jesus died so we could have more than a fleeting fix. He wants us to receive the permanent cure.

Tootle-loo, I'll See You There

Several years ago, when I was a youth pastor, an eighteen-year-old college freshman who had attended my high-school group was buried alive in a construction accident. It took almost seven minutes for rescuers to uncover Brian's head. He was whisked by helicopter to Harborview Hospital, one of the top trauma centers in the country. His throat and windpipe were filled with dirt. After all this time, he was still not getting oxygen.

Rushing to Harborview, I was allowed into the trauma center. Standing a few feet away, I quietly prayed while literally dozens of doctors, nurses, and technicians worked on him. Surrounding his gurney three deep, the trauma team did all they could. After a while, a doctor reported there was almost no chance of Brian surviving, but if he did, he would suffer severe brain damage.

Later that day, several members of our youth group met with Ellie and me at church to pray intensely for an hour or two. Just as we were finishing, Brian's dad called from the hospital to say that Brian was conscious. I could hardly believe it, yet I was overjoyed! Brian went on to make a spectacular recovery—a miraculous recovery. There was no long-term brain damage. The doctors had no explanation. Initially Brian praised God and gave him all the credit. But within a week or two, he changed his tune, claiming his own strength and determination saved him, not God.

I was stunned by his change of heart. I lost touch with Brian within a few years. He went his own way—living life in the fast lane—with lots of parties, women, sports cars, and drugs. What a wasted life after the most amazing miracle

I have ever witnessed. But even an obvious miracle can be discerned only by faith.

This story is just background for saying I do not think you have the strength to beat cancer by yourself. Yet I believe with all my heart that God's strength, love, grace, and presence are fully available to you. Lean on him. I continue to seek a miracle. I sense and expect God's glory will be revealed, whether you're healed or Jesus carries you home. We keep trusting in Christ alone, not just in his power to perform a miracle. Whatever happens, "to live is Christ and to die is gain" (Phil. 1:21).

Expecting something great!
Uncle Don

—

> Praise the LORD, O my soul,
>   and forget not all his benefits—
> who forgives all your sins
>   and heals all your diseases,
> who redeems your life from the pit
>   and crowns you with love and compassion,
> who satisfies your desires with good things
>   so that your youth is renewed like the eagle's.
>   (Ps. 103:2–5)

17

The Big Picture

AFTER Pete's death, his good friend Scott shared a vivid dream, which placed him in a store filled with priceless antiquities. As the proprietor of the shop pointed out the extreme worth of a particular item, Peter appeared on the scene saying, "Scott, that's not valuable." The alarm rang, waking Scott before Pete revealed where the real value lay. Yet, when Peter died, through words and what we witnessed, he showed us the ultimate treasure is found in Jesus.

Cancer taught Peter that the dying process can be ugly and very unpleasant. For him, it included chemotherapy, hospitalization, needles, and suffering—being stripped of strength, vitality, and dignity, as well as the wrenching pain of a thousand good-byes. Death pulled the rug out from under him. He wouldn't graduate from college, get married, have children, or accomplish his goals. Life wasn't turning out the way he'd planned.

Confronted with death, Peter looked to the One who had walked that path before. Isaiah 53 revealed "a man of sorrows, acquainted with bitterest grief" (v. 3 NLT), someone who completely understood Pete's anguish, having died an unbelievably worse death. As Pete yielded his life, Jesus gently guided him on the steep, uphill journey home.

One night I read a passage to Pete. Jesus prayed, "Father, I want these whom you've given me to be with me, so they can see my glory" (John 17:24 NLT).

"Did you hear what Jesus said, Pete?" I asked. "He longs for you to be with him in heaven."

His eyes danced as he responded, "To share his glory—that's amazing." The verse shed new light on dying, helping Peter to see it as a personal invitation to paradise. The big picture was growing more defined.

During his last hours, I marveled at Pete's clear awareness of a reality larger than the agony he suffered. His pain was real, but even more significant was the love, peace, and joy he experienced. Seeing the end of the road and the gates of heaven open and inviting, he heard the voice of God welcoming him home. Nothing could be better; Peter knew it, and wanted us to know it. He had the big picture.

Holding fast to Christ, Pete left this world for heaven. To say his death was gain seems a gross understatement. We were left envious of Pete. Dave said, "I wanted to hold onto his leg and be pulled along." Pete's now with his Lord, who loves him and delights in him. He's home, the place he belongs, his heart's desires met.

⌒

High King of Heaven, my victory won,
May I reach Heaven's joys, O bright Heaven's Sun!
Heart of my own heart, whatever befall,
Still be my Vision, O Ruler of all.

—Dallan Forgaill,
"Be Thou My Vision"

May 28, 1998

Good evening Pete,

As I sit down to offer you encouragement, I think of what I've already written. Perhaps I've made some pretty radical claims in these letters. It might strike some as outlandish, but I believe that we currently reside in the land of the dying, and through Christ are headed to the land of the living.

When I was your age, I felt compelled to investigate whether this belief could be true. The answer depends upon the resurrection of Christ. If Jesus did rise from the dead, he defeated our greatest enemy, death. Those who trust in him are forgiven. God is for us, not against us. Heaven is our ultimate home.

But if Jesus' body decomposed in some Palestinian tomb, then the grave is the last word on life. Death is the final reality, making life meaningless and a mockery of our faith. There is no forgiveness or eternal life. "If we have hope in Christ only for this life, we are the most miserable people in the world" (1 Cor. 15:19 NLT).

Peter, I really wrestled with this issue, discussing it with Christians and atheists. I read books for and against. The more questions I asked, the more I found answers that made sense to me. In the end, I concluded Jesus really is God incarnate, who defeated sin and death through the cross and resurrection.

This world really is the land of the dying. That didn't

take a lot of investigation. Yet my heart said our lives still must have some meaning or purpose. The Bible's explanation seemed to validate my observations. God created human beings to live with him forever. Yet we rejected fellowship with God, wanting to act as our own god, determining what is right and wrong for ourselves. The Bible calls this sin. So God allowed us to go our own way, and this world began to die. We became estranged from God. But God continued to love his rebellious children. In fact, he became one of us in Jesus, dying in order to break the hold of sin and death. Rising from the dead, he returned to heaven to prepare a place for us—the new land of the living.

God has placed eternity in our hearts, causing us to long for more than this decaying world. Jesus is the only way to eternal life.

My search demanded a choice: Do I reject or accept Jesus? Either option required faith. But the evidence and my heart said Jesus rose from the dead. Since those days, that conviction has only deepened. Now Jesus is more than a philosophical truth; he is my Savior and best friend.

Peter, "the fact is that Christ has been raised from the dead. He has become the first of a great harvest of those who will be raised to life again" (1 Cor. 15:20 NLT). Because he lives, we will, too. You and I can say, "For to me, to live is Christ and to die is gain" (Phil. 1:21). Sharing this certainty is the greatest encouragement I can offer you.

I really believe this and know you do, too,
Uncle Don

—

If it is preached that Christ has been raised from the dead, how can some of you say that there is no resurrection of the dead? If there is no resurrection of the dead, then not even Christ has been raised. And if Christ has not been raised, our preaching is useless and so is your faith. . . . But Christ has indeed been raised from the dead, the firstfruits of those who have fallen asleep. (1 Cor. 15:12–14, 20)

18

The Last Fishing Trip

ON a cold, blustery day, a month before Peter died, Andy and Pete set off on their last fishing trip to nearby Cullaby Lake. Borrowing their Aunt Sena's canoe, one of their favorite sports beckoned. Andy had cooked up the idea, and Pete never passed up an opportunity to be with his brother. But this excursion didn't live up to expectations.

Bone tired and dead weary, Peter probably should have stayed home, but he gamely headed for the lake. Not giving in to illness, he paddled until weakness overtook him. Noticing his fatigue, Andy said, "Don't worry, Pete, I'll paddle from here on." Before long, Pete caught the first of several small bass. But not even hauling in the catch brought them the pleasure it once had. Grief dampened their spirits, and the brothers lacked their usual easy banter.

Exhaustion cut the day short; Peter needed to go home. Andy paddled the canoe back to the dock and watched Peter struggle to get out. So whipped he almost staggered, Peter barely made it back to the truck before collapsing into the passenger seat.

They had desired a special time together, wanting to store up memories for the dark days ahead. But that perfect day escaped them, leaving a longing for more than a few enjoyable hours together, and a craving for something better, something permanent.

Twelve months later, Andy returned home and again planned a fishing expedition. Alone, he set out expecting to have a great time.

But images from the past—painful yet cherished—overwhelmed him, calling a halt to fishing that day. Andy couldn't go on, not without Peter. Fishing was temporarily put on the back burner as he reflected upon the bittersweet trip the year before.

Andy's passion for fishing continues. Every year he eagerly waits for opening day. For him, fishing is a reminder there is an eternal land where his hunger for perfection will be fully satisfied. With unbridled joy, Andy will fish with Pete again.

Green pastures are before me, which yet I have not seen.
Bright skies will soon be o'er me, where darkest clouds have been.
My hope I cannot measure, my path to life is free.
My Savior has my treasure, and He will walk with me.

—Anna L. Waring,
"In Heavenly Love Abiding"

May 29, 1998

Dear Pete,

    This morning your parents told me that test results show your cancer has advanced. My heart broke, even though at some level it did not surprise me. I hung up and cried. I still feel like crying all these hours later. Ellie, Laura, and Julie feel the same. Your life affects so many. Whether in living or dying, you are important to God, and he has a plan for you.

    When I visited Hamlet in March, I reminded you that everyone was impressed with your courage and strength following the removal of your eye four years ago. I continue to be impressed. You are an amazing young man! I believe the Lord's power at work in you is becoming even more visible this time around. All of us who love you see the Lord reflected in your life. People will come to faith because of you. You're a vessel to display his greatness.

    I keep praying this means you will be healed. I still believe it's possible as a result of God's miraculous power. But whether you live or die, Christ will accomplish his purpose through you. Your life—even your suffering—has eternal significance. Believe it, Pete. It's true.

    A little girl named Haley lives next door. She asked her mom about heaven after a trip to the local water park. Her mom told her to ask me. Haley started a conversation over the little fence that separates our yards. I'll never forget how she phrased her question: "Don, will there be a Wild Waves in heaven?" It was a profound question. She seemed to be saying, "Could heaven beat Wild Waves?" To her, at that moment, the slides and rides at Wild Waves represented the best this life had to offer. If heaven didn't have it, then maybe it would be better not to go there.

Gulping, I silently prayed for the right words before responding, "I don't know, Haley. But I do know there will be something far better there." And then I paraphrased Paul's words: "I am torn between continuing my life here or going to heaven: I really want to leave and be with Christ, which is better by far" (Phil. 1:23).

That last phrase, "better by far," is the most succinct biblical description of heaven I have found. Here, we are like children making mud pies. Just as they can't compare to your mom's homemade blackberry pies, so the best this world has doesn't hold a candle to heaven. Even what we cherish above all else, family and friends, is a wispy shadow of what our relationships will be in heaven. There will be no conflicts—no misunderstandings, selfish behavior, or jealousy. Friends will never betray or disappoint us. We will be bound together in perfect love.

Your new home will outshine the beauty of Hamlet or the panoramic views of Mount Rainier I love so much. The colors will be more varied and brilliant. The air will be purer; the smells will absolutely delight you. The music of heaven will exceed any heard here. Every earthly pleasure is only a hint of what heaven offers.

There will be wonderful reunions without the forced separation of death. There will be no more war. If volcanic eruptions and storms occur, they will be mighty displays of God's creative abilities, not natural disasters. Perhaps they will be heaven's fireworks, producing amazement, not fear and destruction.

Whatever else heaven is, it isn't boring. You will run like the wind. You will experience marvel after marvel. Best of all, you will meet Jesus face to face. I'm confident you will hear him say, "Well done, Pete. You have been my good and faithful servant." Then you will experience the joy of the Lord in a way that transcends any joy ever known on earth. "To live is Christ and to die is gain" (Phil. 1:21).

Waiting for that day,
Uncle Don

For I live in eager expectation and hope that I will never do anything that causes me shame, but that I will always be bold for Christ, as I have been in the past, and that my life will always honor Christ, whether I live or I die. For to me, living is for Christ, and dying is even better. (Phil. 1:20–21 NLT)

19

More Than I Asked

HUNDREDS of people offered up thousands of prayers for Peter during his illness. These petitions on Peter's behalf played a huge role in readying him for the glories of heaven.

An article, titled "Pray for Pete," written by the sports editor for the Seaside newspaper, encouraged local people to remember how much Peter needed their prayers. Following is a portion of his writing:

> Peter Hill is battling for his life against cancer just three years after representing Seaside High School in both the state championship football game and state championship track meet in the 1994–'95 school year. It would be more than fitting for the community, which Peter, an all-state performer in track and football, pumped so much life into, to do its best to give him a reason to get well and be a living legend. . . .
>
> There is no way that any of us can understand, let alone know, what thoughts Peter and his family are sharing. The best we can do is keep using prayer to support the challenges they are taking on.[1]

The outpouring of prayer from the community humbled us while assisting Peter to his greatest victory ever.

When Pete prayed, he asked for God's will to be accomplished in his life. Death wasn't what he wanted, but he believed God's plans were better than his own. The night he died, Pete's faith had grown until God's will had become his own will. In answering Pete's prayer, God led him home in glory.

Throughout Pete's illness, a steady stream of pleading flowed from my hurt: "God, please hold Pete close to your heart; may he experience your love. Don't let his faith waver or allow him to stumble. Show him your grace. Cause Pete to stand firm—body, soul, and spirit. Make him ready. Help, help, help, help, Lord. Our family needs you." Prayer carried us in our darkest hours.

I asked several friends and my sisters to pray that as Peter died, there would be a hint of a smile on his face, or some other sign that he died not just resigned but eager to meet his Savior. God responded far beyond anything I had imagined possible.

Hungry for God, Pete intensely desired and needed prayer. Dave and I often paraphrased Ephesians 3:16–21 as we prayed for him:

> God, from your glorious, unlimited resources give Pete mighty inner strength through your Holy Spirit. We pray Christ will be more and more at home in his heart as he trusts in you. May Pete's roots go down deep into the soil of your marvelous love. And may he have the power to understand, as all God's children should, how wide, how long, how high, and how deep your love really is. May he experience the love of Christ; though it is so great he will never fully understand it. Then Pete will be filled with the fullness of life and power that comes from you.

We were astonished when God answered this prayer so powerfully.

Many prayed for a miracle, foremost among them was Peter's grandma. She couldn't bear the thought of the alternative and prayed fervently for his healing. The week before he died, a voice woke her from sleep with the words, "I will heal him—in heaven."

With tremendous love and joy, God gave Pete the best: the ultimate, perfect healing. A friend explained to me that she woke to pray for Peter in the still darkness each night during his illness. On the morning of June 14, she arose disturbed, realizing she hadn't prayed for him the previous night. Later in church she discovered why such petitions were no longer necessary: Peter had left his troubles behind as he entered heaven in an awesome display of glory. As we stood by in wonder, all prayers for Pete were answered.

⌁

Haste then on from grace to glory,
Armed by faith, and winged by prayer;
Heaven's eternal days before thee,
God's own hand shall guide thee there.
—Henry F. Lyte,
"Jesus, I My Cross Have Taken"

June 1, 1998

Hi Pete,

It's a cool, cloudy Monday morning. I expected to be on my way to see you today, but last night your mom called, suggesting today would be a bad time to visit. I'm glad she was honest, and I do plan to come next Monday. Sorry you're feeling so lousy.

To say you'd rather be home than in the hospital is a huge understatement. In the hospital you're Peter Hill, a patient; at home you are Pete, son and brother. The hospital offers medical treatment; home offers love and comfort. You're admitted to the hospital, but you belong at home.

Pete, what is the longing of your heart? Do you want to return to Hamlet, or are you starting to yearn for your eternal home in heaven? At Hamlet you will still be housed in your cancer-stricken body. When Jesus takes you to the land of the living, the cancer won't go with you. It stays in the land of the dying.

Paul compares our present bodies to "tents" and the new bodies we will receive in heaven to "houses." I don't mind living in a tent for a few days while backpacking, but I always look forward to the comforts of home. Tents are temporary. In heaven we'll live in "an eternal house." No wonder Paul went on to say, "Meanwhile we groan, longing to be clothed with our heavenly dwelling" (2 Cor. 5:2). Paul didn't have cancer; still he hungered for his heavenly home. We're created for heaven. Our hearts will never be fully satisfied until we're with Jesus.

I identify with the poignant story of missionary Samuel Morrison. Leaving Africa after serving faithfully for many years, his health ruined, he embarked on his final journey home. It turned out Teddy Roosevelt was a passenger on the same ship. Upon arrival in New York, thousands of people crammed the docks, wanting to catch a glimpse of the popular president. A grand celebration with bands and waving flags welcomed Roosevelt. As he walked down the gangplank, a shower of confetti and cheers engulfed the president. A short time later, the elderly missionary walked down the same gangplank. But the bands were silent as he slipped anonymously into the dispersing crowd. "This is so unfair, Lord," he thought. "I've served you for a quarter of a century in Africa, but no one cares. The president was only there a few weeks to hunt animals, and masses turn out to celebrate his return home." In the quietness of his wounded heart, he heard God whisper, "But my dear child, you are not home yet!"

Pete, even if you were in Hamlet, you would not truly be home. Jesus has gone before you to prepare a better home for you, and when the time is right, he'll return to take you there. So we can affirm with all of our being, "To live is Christ and to die is gain" (Phil. 1:21). Live for him while you're confined to this land of the dying, as a way of preparing to be with him in the land of the living.

Longing for our true home,
Uncle Don

—

Now we know that if the earthly tent we live in is destroyed, we have a building from God, an eternal house in heaven, not built by human hands. Meanwhile we groan, longing to be clothed with our heavenly dwelling. (2 Cor. 5:1–2)

20

Rescued from My Island

GRIEF isolated me, set me apart, and cut me off from normal relationships. Pete's cancer consumed all my energy, demanded every emotion, and dominated every thought. Something as ordinary as walking the halls at the school where I work as an educational assistant required physical exertion that was hard to muster. My heart weighed a ton, settling low in my stomach, dragging me down. Watching people going through their daily routines left me feeling marooned, far from everyday life. Illness and the proximity to death placed me on an invisible island.

I needed people to express their awareness of my sorrow. When anyone acknowledged Peter's illness, they helped span the distance to my island. Hugs, inquiries about his health, a pat on the back, little gestures that showed empathy freed me to be a part of a group, emotionally allowing me to join a conversation about happenings not associated with Pete. One friend simply asked, "How are you doing?" Another admitted, "I don't know what to say, other than I'm sorry. Will you join me for a cup of coffee?" When people recognized my situation, they allowed me to smile and enter everyday conversation without feeling like a liar, disloyal to my broken heart.

Silence widened the distance. At times, hurt overwhelmed me to the point I lost perspective, thinking the world should stop turning. My life had crumbled—how could others continue as if nothing earthshaking had happened? Still, underneath my turmoil I realized most people cared, some deeply. Yet fear of saying the wrong thing or of causing the tears to overflow muted their voices.

Eight years after his death, I continue to find comfort when someone speaks of Peter. I don't want my friends to feel compelled to bring him into all conversations, but the occasional, brief remembrance is appreciated. A coworker stopped me outside of school and said, "When I see you, I think of Peter." On Mother's Day a friend greeted me with a hug and the words, "This must be a difficult day for you." These expressions of care filled me with solace, reaching my island. Peter's high school English teacher recently reminded me how remarkable she considered Peter; she still thinks of him often. Her comments brought tears, yet they made my day.

Grief made some friends uncomfortable. As long as we focused on the amazing miracle witnessed when Peter died, everything was fine, but talking about the hole left in my life was not okay. Some have even insinuated that I have a spiritual problem when I feel sad; for them it seems that a Christian's only permissible emotion is joy. Knowing this makes me hesitant to express honest feelings, keeping me firmly entrenched on my island.

Pete's death has taught me that words and actions assist in breaking the isolation that accompanies sorrow. Until Christ completely heals me in heaven, my heart will hurt. Meanwhile, I'm thankful for friends and family who have stood by me through the pain, affirming my loss and listening to me ramble on about Pete. They have helped me back to the mainland.

Rescued from My Island

⌐

Before our Father's throne
We pour our ardent prayers;
Our fears, our hopes, our aims are one
Our comforts and our cares.

We share each other's woes,
Our mutual burdens bear;
And often for each other flows
The sympathizing tear.

—John Fawcett,
"Blest Be the Tie That Binds"

Dear Peter,

I wish I could be with you tomorrow and eat a slice of birthday pie. I'm sorry you won't be able to celebrate your twenty-first birthday the way most people dream of, but I'm glad you are at Hamlet, not in the hospital. Hamlet is so much a part of you, your family, and your history.

Hamlet is the only home you know. You've fished the creeks, hunted in the hills, and worked in the woods. Hamlet is your legacy, almost part of your DNA. Homesteading in isolated, rugged country, your great-grandfather and his two brothers were the earliest settlers in the Hamlet valley, the first white men to see the steep hillsides covered with old-growth fir and the rivers thick with salmon. Your great-granddad cleared the land and planted crops, building his house with hand-hewn lumber.

Twenty-six years ago, your granddad retired early and moved back to the homestead house with your grandma. In the middle of a frigid winter, I helped move their first load of belongings. Deep snow blanketed the forest, the creek was frozen over; we broke ice to get drinking water. There was no electricity. The only heat came from the fireplace. Through hard work, your grandparents restored Hamlet as the family home.

A few years later, your dad and mom built your present house a few hundred yards from the old Hamlet house.

Andy was a toddler and Sam a preschooler. You were born the following year. Your dad worked as a state forester for a while, before quitting to work with your granddad on the family homestead. You are Hamlet born and raised. And one day, Hamlet will be inherited by the next generation—yours and your brothers'.

Yet earthly inheritances are never fully secure. If researchers developed an expensive new treatment that promised a cure for cancer, without hesitation your parents and grandparents would sell Hamlet to save your life. Your earthly inheritance would be lost. But nothing can take away your heavenly inheritance. It was paid for in Jesus' blood and insured by his resurrection. It's yours forever.

The priceless inheritance kept in heaven for you is more than just a house or place. It's the identity and privileges of being a child of God. The Bible says "we are heirs—heirs of God and co-heirs with Christ" (Rom. 8:17). The New Living Translation puts it this way: "Since we are his children, we will share his treasures—for everything God gives to his Son, Christ, is ours, too. But if we are to share his glory, we must also share his suffering."

Everything that belongs to Jesus will also belong to you, even his suffering and glory. You are an adopted son, sharing equally in the family inheritance.

Why did God adopt you? The answer is simple; he loves you, Peter. So your true home is in heaven, where your inheritance is waiting for you. It's better than anything you could ever inherit in this land of the dying. Paul understood this and so could say, "For to me, to live is Christ and to die is gain" (Phil. 1:21). And you, too, understand it—the best is yet to come.

I love you nephew,
Uncle Don

Now we live with a wonderful expectation because Jesus Christ rose again from the dead. For God has reserved a priceless inheritance for his children. It is kept in heaven for you, pure and undefiled, beyond the reach of change and decay. And God, in his mighty power, will protect you until you receive this salvation, because you are trusting him. (1 Peter 1:3–5 NLT)

21

Filled to Overflowing

THE world's hold on Peter lessened as his cancer progressed. When hospitalized in Portland, Andy asked Pete if he wanted a radio to help pass the long, miserable days. With feeling Pete said, "No, definitely not." As his relationship with God deepened, worldly pastimes lost their importance. The things Pete once found pleasure in—music, televised sports, books (except C. S. Lewis and Scripture)—no longer claimed his interest. As he sought Christ like never before, unseen internal changes occurred, leaving room for the Holy Spirit to work in wondrous ways. The external results were astonishing.

The day before Peter died, my brother, Don, excitedly repeated several times, "Char, can't you feel it? I think God is going to heal Pete." Don sensed the Holy Spirit at work in Pete's life and expected something remarkable to happen. Indeed, the remarkable happened, but not the way we had at first hoped.

In his last hours, as Peter freely yielded his life, the Holy Spirit coursed through him. The godly attributes from Galatians 5—love, joy, peace, patience, kindness, goodness, faithfulness, gentleness, and self-control—were revealed to the thirteen people mesmerized by the supernatural events unfolding before us.

As I sat on the edge of Peter's bed with my hand on him, *love* seemed to pour from him. He loved us in a way I'd never experienced before: totally, freely, unselfishly, spontaneously, sincerely. Love bubbled up and sloshed over.

Exhilarating, wonderful *joy* overpowered Peter and swept him up. Wings of joy carried him home while he exuberantly shouted, "Woo hoo!"

Deep *peace* filled Pete as he assured us, "I'm okay, don't worry about me." Being in his presence, we couldn't doubt the depth of his peace and contentment. No words or actions showed the least bit of anxiety in spite of his circumstances.

Patiently, Peter waited for God to take him to the Promised Land. He had seen God, and God promised him Jesus would soon come for him. Peter said, "I'm waiting. Christ is returning for me."

With tremendous *kindness* Pete expressed his love, seeking to comfort and encourage each of us before he left. His heartfelt concern was for our well-being.

Earlier that evening Pete had seen God and testified, "God is good. God is very good." That *goodness* splashed over onto Peter, transforming him, making him ready for heaven.

Pete died in *faith*, sharing his love of God. Speaking with conviction, more than anything he wanted us to know, "Christ is the answer."

Gently yet earnestly he spoke his last words to us, "I love you all. I love everybody in this room. God bless you all. God bless you all."

And Pete's *self-control* was impressive. Every breath he took seemed measured. In the worst of circumstances, he remained undemanding, thinking of others, always in control.

Memories of that incredible night continue to overwhelm me. Pete, overflowing with the fruits of the Spirit, displayed God's amazing love and power. Nothing has opened my eyes more to God's unending goodness and heaven's glory than Peter's final hours on earth. Truly, "God is good. God is *very* good."

Have Thine own way, Lord! Have Thine own way!
Hold o'er my being absolute sway!
Fill with Thy Spirit till all shall see,
Christ only, always, living in me.

—Adelaide A. Pollard,
"Have Thine Own Way, Lord"

Hi Pete,

Sorry I couldn't be with you on your twenty-first birthday. Ellie and I prayed you would have enough energy to enjoy the festivities. But cancer probably cast a shadow over your celebration just as it does over every other part of your life.

As you know, the course of cancer cannot be predicted. About the time you think things are improving, a new infection pops up and sets you back. Pete, one unexpected but positive side effect of your illness is that it may cause your heart to ache for heaven. Perhaps you are already feeling this heavenly homesickness, longing for a place where cancer cannot intrude.

Yet going to heaven—your true home—involves facing the unknown. Part of what makes a strange place scary is not knowing anyone. Journeying to a place where friends are waiting reduces anxiety. Better yet is returning home to the arms of loved ones. Their sure welcome leaves no room for worry and floods you with anticipation.

My first semester of graduate school in St. Louis was hard. I didn't know a single soul and quickly developed a bad case of homesickness. Loneliness overwhelmed me as I struggled to learn Greek and Hebrew. I wanted to be home where I was known, loved, and where I belonged. After finals, I jumped in my old '67 Plymouth and headed to Michigan for Christmas break. Aunt Mary and her family had moved there a few months before. Because Mary and I are close, I looked forward to spending the holidays with her in Ann Arbor. Yet I was traveling to a strange place.

The drive was long and arduous. I chose a route that took me around Chicago, then east across the state of Michigan to Ann Arbor. By the time I crossed the state line into Michigan, night had fallen, and the first snowflakes floated down. Before long, I found myself in a blizzard. I drove through the deepening snow, barely able to see beyond the hood of the car. Snow flew at me mile after mile, hour after hour.

What seemed like an eternity later, I pulled up to Mary's house. It was after midnight, and all the houses were dark except hers. The porch light was on with light streaming from the living room windows. I trudged through the driving snow to the front steps and looked in. Mary and John sat in wingback chairs pulled before a roaring fire. My heart soared—not only had I found the right house, but they were waiting to welcome me to the warmth of their love and fire. I will never forget that night.

I kept going through the blizzard because I knew Mary would be there to welcome me at the end of the journey. Pete, Jesus is waiting to meet you at the end of your journey home. It will be far better than anything you can imagine. So whether it's sooner or later, live in anticipation of meeting the One who gave his life for you. The light is on as he waits for you with open arms. Like the apostle Paul, you can say with confidence and joy, "For to me, to live is Christ and to die is gain" (Phil. 1:21).

Longing for home,
Uncle Don

—

"When everything is ready, I will come and get you, so that you will always be with me where I am. And you know where I am going and how to get there."

"No, we don't know, Lord," Thomas said. "We haven't any idea where you are going, so how can we know the way?"

Jesus told him, "I am the way, the truth, and the life. No one can come to the Father except through me." (John 14:3–6 NLT)

22

SITTING on the couch, Peter looked down at his scrawny, emaciated legs. He shook his head in distaste and sadly commented, "They're ugly, aren't they?" Those legs epitomized the havoc cancer was wreaking on Pete. Once defined and muscular, carrying him so capably, they now miserably failed him.

As Pete and I read from Isaiah, he found reason to believe better things were coming.

> Even youths grow tired and weary,
>   and young men stumble and fall;
> but those who hope in the LORD
>   will renew their strength.
> They will soar on wings like eagles;
>   they will run and not grow weary,
>   they will walk and not be faint.
> (Isa. 40:30–31)

Hearing these verses kindled new hope in Peter. They sparked his imagination as his heart began to yearn for heaven. Pete marveled at the thought of taking wing and soaring. "Wow, imagine flying," he mused. My fun-loving son dreamed of gliding over mountaintops, swooping and tumbling through the skies, freer than the eagles.

Peter knew running, setting records in the 400-meter dash, one of the hardest, most painful races. At the 300-meter mark, the roof caves in—every breath labored, never enough air, legs like lead, muscles burning and screaming for relief. Finishing is a matter of will, forcing the body to do what it feels it can't. After reading Isaiah, Pete exclaimed, "You can run without getting tired? Awesome!" Excitedly, he talked of the day these feats would become realities.

When God called him home, Peter flew—strong, free, and bursting with joy; leaving us breathless, longing to follow—the promises from Isaiah fulfilled at last.

So, Pete, I'm consoled with the vision of the day we will meet again. Together, we'll effortlessly run the mountaintops in glorious, carefree abandon; laughing and romping, bowing down in endless praise. *"Let's go! Let's go! Woo hoo!"*

⌒

Just a few more weary days and then, I'll fly away;
To a land where joys shall never end, I'll fly away;
I'll fly away, O glory, I'll fly away;
When I die, Hallelujah, by and by, I'll fly away.
—Albert E. Brumley,
"I'll Fly Away"[1]

(Note: Peter died before receiving this last letter from his uncle.)

June 11, 1998

Dear Peter,

I arrived home from my visit with you about thirty minutes ago. The drive was peaceful, giving me lots of time to pray and think about you. Every day your faith grows stronger as your body gets weaker. I don't know how this will turn out, but still I pray for your complete healing. A sense of expectancy that God is going to do something wonderful continues to fill me.

My letters often reflect contrasting truths. I pray for your healing, but I speak about dying. My comments express the conviction that we are only prepared to live when we are first prepared to die. The apostle Paul stated this truth in the verse you know so well: "To live is Christ and to die is gain" (Phil. 1:21).

Paul, locked in a prison cell, condemned to die, wrote his second letter to Timothy—the man he led to Christ and loved like a son. The letter was his last good-bye and expressed the desires of his heart. Without fear or regrets, he declared, "The time of my death is near. I have fought a good fight, I have finished the race, and I have remained faithful" (2 Tim. 4:6-7 NLT).

It had been a hard road home for Paul, but he never quit. He persevered to the end. He kept the faith. He gave it his best shot. Wholeheartedly, Paul was looking forward. Still believing to die was gain, he was ready to move on.

Anticipating his arrival in the land of the living,

Paul asserted, "Now the prize awaits me—the crown of righteousness that the Lord . . . will give me on that great day" (2 Tim. 4:8 NLT). Paul fully expected that, when he arrived in heaven, he would receive his reward—his crown and a commendation from his Lord. He knew his homecoming would be a joyous event.

So as I continue praying for your healing, I also want to congratulate you, Peter, on a race well run. You've never given up; you've given your all. The prize is waiting whenever you cross the finish line, just as it was for Paul. In high school, you repeatedly won the Iron Man award for courage and dedication. If it were up to me, you would win the most inspirational award for courageous faith. In your weakness, you have leaned on God, and the Lord has given you his strength and peace. Your example both challenges and inspires me. What joy waits on that great day! Feeling the Lord's arms around you, seeing the approval in his eyes, and receiving your prize will be the sweetest moment of your life.

It's really all about Jesus, Pete, whether you live or die at this time. He is the one who helps you live well and then die well. May his glory be revealed in your life and in your death because "to live is Christ and to die is gain" (Phil. 1:21).

Joyfully in Christ, yet with tears,
Uncle Don

On Wings like Eagles

You will keep on guiding me with your counsel,
    leading me to a glorious destiny.
Whom have I in heaven but you?
    I desire you more than anything on earth.
My health may fail, and my spirit may grow weak,
    but God remains the strength of my heart;
    he is mine forever.

(Ps. 73:24–26 NLT)

The Party Begins

IN Seaside Hospital, completing his most grueling race with his eyes riveted on the goal, Peter cried out, "It's more beautiful than you can ever imagine!" The joy of victory made the months of pain, hospitalization, and tearful good-byes fall into place. Pete was receiving the greatest prize ever given—heaven.

In my imagination, the scene continues to unfold. I see Jesus at the finish line, urging Peter on, thrilled with his sprint to the end. As Pete breaks the tape, Christ wraps him in a huge bear hug, and then to Pete's utter amazement, places a crown on Peter's head.

Lost in wonder, Pete throws his crown at his Lord's feet, joyfully bowing down in love and adoration before the King of kings. Awash with gratitude and awe for the one who died for him, Peter is astounded to experience Jesus' total delight and approval. Taking Pete's hand, raising him to his feet, Christ returns Pete's crown with these marvelous words: "Well done, Pete. Well done my dear, faithful servant and friend. Welcome home!" Turning to the grandstand, laughing aloud with pleasure, Christ holds Pete's arms high above his head in triumph, enticing the cheering crowd to join the celebration. Unbelievably, Jesus heaps glory upon Peter! The snowballing of everything good, both imagined and beyond imagination, has started. From here on, it will only get better.

From the crowd, Pete spies two beautiful people rushing to greet him. Joyfully, he recognizes these strong, bright, and ageless individuals as his grandparents. Excitement bubbles through him, making him more alive and free than he ever thought possible. Peter perceives just a glimmer of how exhilarating the adventure will be. The party begins!

My mind's picture floods me with anticipation, knowing the reality of heaven will fulfill my longings in ways I can't begin to fathom.

> No eye has seen, no ear has heard,
> and no mind has imagined
> what God has prepared
> for those who love him.
> (1 Cor. 2:9 NLT)

Epilogue

Dear Readers,

Today would have been Peter's thirtieth birthday. June 13, eight days from now, will mark the ninth anniversary of his death. I miss him. The tears still fall. He's left an indelible mark on my life.

I recall shooting baskets with Andy and him in front of my parents' Seaside home. Pete had just turned seventeen and his face was still bandaged from the surgery to remove his eye. Andy and I were both talking trash and enjoying our advantage over Pete in a game of "21." I won—the only time I ever beat Peter in any athletic endeavor!

Less than four years later, my sister Mary called from Michigan with the news that Peter's cancer had returned. I hung up the phone sobbing. The next day at Hamlet, Pete looked and acted fine, making it awkward to know what to say. Words failed me. Talking trash on the basketball court was easier than talking about life and death.

Epilogue

I needed a way to express what really mattered, things I found hard to say in person. A month later I started the first of many letters to Pete, tears streaming, as they did each time I wrote to him. My intent was to help Pete, but putting it on paper also helped me. Writing became my way of connecting with Peter—drawing us closer together. Without embarrassment I could tell him I loved him.

How ironic—I attempted to coach Pete during his last months with us, but Pete ended up teaching me. I repeatedly wrote about living for Christ and viewing death as gain. Pete did it. He demonstrated that it's attainable for an ordinary guy like me. It's within my reach. I don't have to become a saint first. I merely have to trust and believe, "For to me, to live is Christ and to die is gain" (Phil. 1:21).

I'm sorry I wasn't there to witness the victory and wonder as Pete died—to experience a glimpse of the grandeur, glory, and beauty to come as Peter flew home. But even though I wasn't there, knowing what happened has helped me live with a greater awareness of the eternal. Peter's death has made me homesick for heaven.

The morning after Pete died, I stood before my congregation and, between sobs, related the awe inspiring events. Those in attendance shared my grief and comforted me with their hugs. In the months and years that followed, my congregation has continued to hear stories about Pete in sermons, articles, and personal conversations. I have shared about Pete in hospital rooms, funeral homes, and everywhere I've gone. Pete's story has become my story.

Three years ago while visiting a community devastated by AIDS in Swaziland, Africa, I was invited to preach. What could I offer them in their poverty, pain, and grief? I spoke simply from Philippians 1:21, tying it to Peter's life and death. It bridged the gulf between our differing cultures and languages. Hope is a language everyone understands.

Peter helped me clarify my goals. It's not complicated. I want to live well and I want to die well. For me, living well means to live with, like, and for Christ. Jesus is my all in all. The closer I get to him the more I want to be in his presence. I look forward to that wondrous day when the curtain is lifted for me and, like Pete, I meet Jesus face-to-face.

In the meantime, I live in joyous anticipation,
Don

> You will show me the way of life,
>   granting me the joy of your presence
>   and the pleasures of living with you forever.
>   (Ps. 16:11 NLT)

Notes

Chapter 1: Every Chapter Better Than the One Before
1. Wilson Rawls, *Summer of the Monkeys* (Garden City, NY: Doubleday, 1976).
2. C. S. Lewis, *The Last Battle* (New York: Macmillan, 1956), 173–74.

Chapter 2: Hamlet
1. Charles Wesley, "And Can It Be That I Should Gain?"

Chapter 6: Acceptance
1. Joseph M. Stowell, *Reclaiming a Passion for What Endures: Eternity* (Chicago: Moody Press, 1995), 9.

Chapter 7: The Pain of Loving
1. C. S. Lewis, *The Problem of Pain* (San Francisco: Harper-SanFrancisco, 2001), 91.

Chapter 9: Fear
1. Rick Warren, *The Purpose Driven Life* (Grand Rapids: Zondervan, 2002), 45–46.

Chapter 10: Infinite Joy
1. C. S. Lewis, *Letters to Malcolm: Chiefly on Prayer* (New York: Harcourt, Brace & Jovanovich, 1964), 93.

Chapter 13: Missing You
1. Terra's essay has been edited for publication.
2. The names of the brothers in this story have been changed to protect their privacy.

Chapter 19: More Than I Asked
1. Brian Liebenstein, "Pray for Pete," *Seaside Signal*, May 28, 1998. Used by permission.

Chapter 22: On Wings Like Eagles
1. © Copyright 1932 in "Wonderful Message" by Hartford Music Co. Renewed 1960 by Albert E. Brumley & Sons/SESAC (admin. by ICG). All rights reserved. Used by permission.